AVID

READER

PRESS

ALSO BY STEPHEN MARCHE

The Unmade Bed
The Hunger of the Wolf
Love and the Mess We're In
How Shakespeare Changed Everything
Shining at the Bottom of the Sea
Raymond and Hannah

THE NEXT CIVIL WAR

Dispatches from the American Future

STEPHEN MARCHE

AVID READER PRESS

New York   London   Toronto   Sydney   New Delhi

AVID READER PRESS
An Imprint of Simon & Schuster, Inc.
1230 Avenue of the Americas
New York, NY 10020

First Avid Reader Press hardcover edition January 2022

AVID READER PRESS and colophon are trademarks of Simon & Schuster, Inc.

For information about special discounts for bulk purchases, please contact Simon &
Schuster Special Sales at 1-866-506-1949 or business@simonandschuster.com.

The Simon & Schuster Speakers Bureau can bring authors to your live event. For
more information or to book an event contact the Simon & Schuster Speakers
Bureau at 1-866-248-3049 or visit our website at www.simonspeakers.com.

Interior design by Carly Loman

Manufactured in the United States of America

10 9 8 7 6 5 4 3 2 1

Library of Congress Cataloging-in-Publication Data has been applied for.

ISBN 978-1-9821-2321-5
ISBN 978-1-9821-2323-9 (ebook)

To Elijah and Aviva

At what point then is the approach of danger to be expected? I answer, if it ever reach us, it must spring up amongst us. It cannot come from abroad. If destruction be our lot, we must ourselves be its author and finisher. As a nation of freemen, we must live through all time, or die by suicide.

—Abraham Lincoln

Contents

An Introduction to the Immediate Future of the United States

The United States is coming to an end. The question is how. Every government, every business, every person alive will be affected by the answer.

The unimaginable has become everyday in America. Buffoonish mobs desecrating the US Capitol building, tear gas and tanks on the streets of Washington, DC, running battles between protestors and militias, armed rebels attempting to kidnap sitting governors, uncertainty about the peaceful transition of power—reading about them in another country, you would think a civil war had already begun. The United States is descending into the kind of sectarian conflict usually found in poor countries with histories of violence, not the world's most enduring democracy and largest economy. The fall has been sudden. A decade ago, American stability and global supremacy were a given. The memory of September 11 led to regular mass demonstrations of national unity. The United States was synonymous with the glory of democracy. No longer. Solidarity has dissolved. The American system has become a case study of paralysis. Political violence is on the rise.

The next civil war in America won't look like a civil war in a smaller country. The United States is fragile but enormous. Its military might remains unparalleled. Its economy determines the health of the global economy. If the American Republic falls, democracy as the leading political system in the world falls. If democracy falls, the peace and security of the global order falls. No one will escape the consequences.

The Likelihood of a Civil War

Retired US Army colonel Peter Mansoor, professor of military history at The Ohio State University, is a veteran of the Iraq war who now studies the insurgencies of the past. He doesn't have any difficulty picturing a contemporary American equivalent to civil wars elsewhere. "It would not be like the first civil war, with armies maneuvering on the battlefield," he says. "I think it would very much be a free-for-all, neighbor on neighbor, based on beliefs and skin colors and religion. And it would be horrific."

In a poll taken in the aftermath of Trump's election, 31 percent of American voters predicted a second civil war would occur within five years. In *Foreign Policy*, a panel of national security experts assessed the chances of a civil war over the next ten to fifteen years. The answers ranged from 5 percent to 95 percent. The consensus stood at 35 percent. In the eyes of the expert class and ordinary Americans alike, the odds of a civil war in the near future are about the same as drawing ten or higher from a pack of cards.

That estimation was only "over the next ten to fifteen years" though. The pressure is mounting, and the forces fraying American unity—the hyper-partisan politics, the environmental degradation, the widening inequality—are growing. A 2019 poll from Georgetown University asked Americans how close to "the edge of a civil war" their country was, on a scale from 0 to 100. The aggregate of their answers was 67.23, so almost exactly two-thirds of the way.

The technical definition of a civil war, according to the Centre for the Study of Civil War at the Peace Research Institute Oslo, is a thousand combatant deaths within a year. The definition of civil strife starts at twenty-five deaths within a year. In the United States in 2019, domestic anti-government extremists killed forty-two people; in 2018 they killed fifty-three people; in 2017, thirty-seven; in 2016, seventy-two; and in 2015, seventy. By this definition, America is already in a state of civil strife, on the threshold of civil war.

The United States as a Complex, Cascading System

There is never a single cause to any civil war. A huge number of factors contribute to the slide of a peaceful prosperous society into violence. The interaction is turbulent, which is why stable scenarios seem to descend into chaos out of nowhere. The complex cascading nature of the system explains why the unimaginable keeps happening.

The unimaginable does not mean the unpredictable. The collapse will arrive sooner and more suddenly than anybody expects, but it won't come as a surprise. America is cracking apart at a moment when the ability to see the cracks spreading has attained unprecedented clarity. NASA recently reported that its climate change modeling has been accurate to within one-twentieth of a degree. The detailed precision of the models as much as the quality of the prediction is extraordinary. When—not if—a Category 1, 2, or 3 hurricane hits New York, the model makers know, to the street, which parts of the city will be rendered uninhabitable. The electoral models of political partisanship have become more effective than their creators can acknowledge: one group of political scientists refused to believe their own program when it told them that Trump would be elected. Such a forecast seemed too outlandish. The contours of economic inequality have never been so thoroughly drawn, their consequences on democracy never so fully understood. Scholars of civil war, used to analyzing conflicts abroad, now see their established patterns replicating themselves identically in the world's richest country, home to the most powerful military in human history.

History books on the subjects of civil wars usually open with chapters about the lead-up to conflict. In the case of the United States, that chapter could be written today. Economic and environmental instability worsens every year. The fruits of the country accrue only to those at the very top. The government, whose legitimacy is never established to the satisfaction of all parties, cannot be relied on. Faith in institutions of all kinds is declining. National purpose is withering. National solidarity is eroding. The government increasingly cannot, even when given clear mandates, respond to its people's will. Political gamesmanship overrides any and all other governmental concerns. Of the last four presidents, two have faced extensive impeachment proceedings. Two elections of the past four have seen the popular winner defeated by an arcane system inherited from the eighteenth century. The judiciary is dogmatic and hardening to the point where the law barely holds meaning outside of the political context of the courts' application. Mass murders are nightly news. Ordinary Americans refuse to listen to authorities, even on questions as important to their survival as public health.

America has lived for 160 years with a half-settled myth of unity. All such myths are fragile. Even the most long-established national identities, the most ancient fusions of peoples and creeds, can dissolve with shocking speed. Before sectarian hatred consumed Iraq, before 2006, the country had a relatively high Shi'a-Sunni intermarriage rate. The supposedly permanent and intractable religious rift was a relic from antiquity. Then it wasn't.

Wherever government fails, whenever the peaceful transition of power breaks down, restoring an orderly democracy takes nothing short of a miracle. America won't be any different. When Democrats feel that they cannot find representation, when Republicans feel that they cannot find representation, the government becomes just another resource to control. Outrage feeds all-consuming cycles of revenge. People retreat into tribes. Once the stability of power goes, it's easy to come up with excuses to murder your neighbors.

The Inciting Incidents

The dispatches that follow are based on the best available models with established predictive capacities. They are more than educated guesses. But the inciting incidents are another matter. They are works of consciously thorough imagination.

Complex, cascading systems are abstract. They don't show human costs. In each of the dispatches that follow, I have imagined an inciting incident to show the human cost. My inspiration was *The Effects of Nuclear War*, a 1979 product of the Office of Technology Assessment, acting on a request from the Senate Committee on Foreign Relations, and arguably the most influential piece of fiction in history. *The Effects of Nuclear War* grew into the miniseries *The Day After*. *The Day After* converted "abstract measures of strategic power" into comprehensible terms, imagining the fallout from nuclear war based on the best available science. Ronald Reagan, in his diaries, cited *The Day After* as a main inspiration behind the Intermediate-Range Nuclear Forces Treaty.

Today's crisis requires prediction because so many people do not want to see what is unfolding in front of their eyes. At the same time, the future is inherently unpredictable. Nobody could have known that an employee at Cup Foods in Minneapolis would report a counterfeit $20 bill and that when the police arrived to investigate the incident an officer named Derek Chauvin would drag a Black man named George Floyd out of a car and, in the process of restraining him, kneel on his neck for seven minutes and forty-six seconds, ignoring more than twenty pleas to allow him to breathe. Nobody could have predicted that plainclothes officers would mistakenly enter the home of Breonna Taylor and kill her. Still less could anyone know that these particular incidents of police brutality, rather than the literally thousands of others, would spark massive protests across the United States. But anyone paying attention could easily have known that the militarization of America's police forces has been underway for decades, that the police in the United States shoot their own citizens at rates that vary between three and thirty times more than the police in other countries, that large swaths of the Black population do not regard the police as legitimate stewards of justice, and that protest movements against police brutality had been gaining momentum since the Obama administration. Breonna Taylor was one of forty-eight Black women shot by police in the United States since 2015. Her name, the particular circumstances of her death—these facts were unpredictable. But not the event itself and not its aftermath. It is entirely predictable now that another incident of police brutality will occur and just as predictable that there will be riots in its wake.

The Point of View of the Dispatches

My nationality gives me a specific advantage in describing an imminent American collapse. Civil conflict forces people to choose sides and their perspective is shaped by the side they've chosen. Confusion precedes any civil conflict. Being Canadian, I am outside that particular confusion.

Canada is the Horatio to America's Hamlet, a close and sympathetic and mostly irrelevant witness to the grand dramatics on the other side of the border. I am a foreigner who has lived in the United States, who works in the United States, who loves the United States. While I'm pretty much in the dead center on the political spectrum of my own country, I don't want to hide the fact that on policy questions my underlying assumptions would be considered liberal by most Americans. I live in a country where socialized medicine and gun control are taken for granted, even by conservatives.

Increasingly, though, being Democrat or Republican is a tribal identification rather than a commitment to particular policies. And I am not of either tribe. As I have crisscrossed the United States to see the conditions on the ground, meeting with white nationalists and Black Lives Matter protestors, with gun sellers and the mothers of mass shooting victims, it has all been equally foreign, the flyover states and the coastal elites, the North and the South. They're all other countries to me. The experts who have informed these dispatches—military leaders, law enforcement officials, agricultural specialists, environmentalists, historians, political scientists—inhabit a wide range on the political spectrum. Many are lifelong Republicans. Nearly half would describe themselves as conservative. I did not strive for a diversity of viewpoints. The people who know what they're talking about come from both sides. They serve larger interests than partisan politics. This book reflects that knowledge and those interests.

The Trump Distraction

You already have feelings about Donald Trump, one way or the other. He is either the last defender of American greatness or a fundamental threat to US democracy. He is either a fighter for traditional American values or a criminal with nothing more than personal impunity for motivation. It doesn't particularly matter which you believe. Trump is far less meaningful than either side understands. The smartest thing he himself ever said about his political career was in a 2017 press conference: "I didn't come along and divide this country. This country was seriously divided before I got here." Trump is, at most, a symptom.

It is essential to recognize this hard fact: if Hillary Clinton had been elected in 2016, all the forces pointing toward the fall of the Republic would be no less powerful than they are right now. Those forces—the hyper-partisanship, the bifurcation of the country into blue and red, the violent loathing for the federal government, the economic unsustainability, the incipient crises in the food supply and urban environmental security, the rise of the hard-right anti-government patriot militias—are the subject of this book. The American experiment was never designed to face what the United States is about to face. No matter who is president, that reality will not change.

Joe Biden's victory speech in the 2020 election announced "a time to heal." It was wishful thinking. Even as the president-elect tried to gesture toward reconciliation, the sitting president wouldn't concede. American liberals in the major cities retain a kind of desperate faith in their country's institutions that amounts nearly to delusion. Americans have taught themselves for 250 years that their country, in its ideals and systems, is the solution to history. It is tough, under those conditions, to accept being just another of history's half perpetrators, half victims.

The hope of a Biden restoration is a faint hope indeed. Barack Obama's presidency was based on what we will, out of politeness, call an illusion of national purpose. He articulated the idea most passionately, most purely, during his keynote address at the 2004 Democratic Convention: "There is not a liberal America and a conservative America—there is the United States of America. There is not a Black America and a White America and Latino America and Asian America—there's the United States of America." It was a beautiful vision. It was also a fantasy. There is very much a red America and a blue America. They occupy different societies with different values, and their political parties are emissaries of that difference.

Unfortunately, America appears to have entered a self-defeating loop, in which the collapsing system prevents reforms to the system itself. Congress can't even agree to investigate violent extremists who attacked its own place of business and threatened the members' own lives. After the Trump years, the Democrats have attempted to salve the wounds inflicted on American institutions, but they remain overwhelmingly committed to the old ways, to the United States they grew up in. One way of reading the current political situation is that Republicans have only come to realize the collapse of the institutions before Democrats. Meanwhile, the window to keep America democratic is closing.

Party politics is mostly a distraction at this point. That's not to excuse the anti-democratic actions of elected officials. In 2021, Oregon representative Mike Nearman was expelled from the state house of representatives because he opened a locked door for the rioters who stormed the Oregon State Capitol. The Republican Party now has an elected wing and an armed militant wing. The point is that the parties and the people in the parties no longer matter much one way or the other. Blaming one side offers a perverse species of hope: "If only more moderate Republicans were in office" . . . "If only bipartisanship could be restored to what it was." Such hopes are not only reckless but irresponsible. The problem is not who is in power but the structures of power. The US system is an archaic mode of government totally unsuited to the realities of the twenty-first century. It needs reforms to its foundational systems, not just new faces.

The United States has burned before. The Vietnam War, the civil rights protests, the assassination of JFK and MLK, Watergate—all were national catastrophes that remain in living memory. But the United States has never faced an institutional crisis quite like the one it is facing now. Trust in the institutions was much higher during the sixties and seventies. The Civil Rights Act had the broad support of both parties. JFK's murder was mourned collectively as a national tragedy. The Watergate scandal, in hindsight, was evidence of the system working. The press reported presidential crimes. Americans took the press seriously. The political parties felt they needed to respond to the reported corruption. You could not make one of those statements today with any confidence. The American political system has become so overwhelmed by anger that even the most basic tasks of government are increasingly impossible. The legal system grows less legitimate by the day. Trust in government at all levels is in free fall or, like Congress with approval ratings hovering around 10 percent, cannot fall any lower. None of this is a prediction, a thought experiment. All of it has already happened. Inside the ruins of the old order, bright flames of pure rage are blossoming.

The Stakes of the Conflict

This book is a warning. Civil wars are total wars laced with atrocities, fought not between professional soldiers but between populations. Insurgent conflicts are wars of meaning, conflicts in which the ideals and communal vision of a country have rotted away. The nature of war against insurgents is so vicious exactly because meaning is at stake: When you are fighting for freedom and your soul, what won't you do?

America was founded with the motto "Out of Many One." If the One fails, a multitude of different factions will emerge out of it: the Black and the white, the North and the South, the coasts and the heartland, Jews, Christians, Muslims, Hindus, Mormons, Scientologists, the Nation of Islam, fifty states, the Seminoles and the Sioux and the Blackfoot and the Comanche, immigrants from every other country on earth. You could, if you wanted, fracture America 327 million different ways.

The forces tearing America apart are both radically modern and as old as the country itself. All that is swelling to the surface now has been lurking underneath for decades, if not from the beginning. Bloody revolution and the threat of secession are essential to the American experiment. America has always been subject to quick, radical change. The question is not whether the United States' factions will descend into conflict, or even what that conflict will look like, but which America will emerge victorious from that conflict.

The Desire Not to See What's Coming

In a sense, the crisis has already arrived. Only the inciting incidents are pending. In America's first civil war, Buchanan's State of the Union address preceded the war itself by five months. But his declaration—that secession was unlawful but that he couldn't constitutionally do anything about it—marked the moment when America split and the war became inevitable. From then on, the country operated by two separate political systems, two legal systems. The country cracked before it divided.

On the eve of America's first civil war, the most intelligent, the most informed, the most dedicated people in the country could not foresee its arrival. Even when Confederate soldiers began their bombardment of Fort Sumter on April 12, 1861, nobody believed that the first civil war was inevitable. The Confederate president, Jefferson Davis, declared the event, in which nobody died, "either the beginning of a fearful war, or the end of a political contest." It was both, and neither. The war had begun earlier. The political contest continued long after.

In Washington, in the winter of 1861, Henry Adams, the grandson of John Quincy Adams, declared that "not one man in America wanted the civil war, or expected or intended it." South Carolina senator James Chesnut Jr., who did more than most to bring on the advent of the catastrophe, promised to drink all the blood spilled in the entire conflict. The common wisdom at the time was that he would have to drink "not a thimble." The North was so unprepared for the war they had no weapons.

At what exact point did the first civil war become inevitable? That question is so tantalizing because it's so unanswerable. The presence of delegates from Georgia in South Carolina was necessary for the South to find its collective courage for secession, and the presence of the Georgian delegates was to celebrate the completion of a railroad between the two states. "If the Charleston and Savannah Railroad had happened to be completed a month earlier or later, might disunion have come at a different time, and/or in another form, or even not at all?" asks William W. Freehling in *The Road to Disunion*. Even a month's delay in a single railroad might have kept hundreds of thousands Americans from dying.

The closer to an event, the more avoidable everything seems. If Lincoln had not been elected, would there have been a war? George Custer, then a cadet at West Point, remembered seeing Southerners heading to the steamboat landing to join their states: "Too far off to exchange verbal adieux, even if military discipline had permitted it, they caught sight of me as step by step I reluctantly paid the penalty of offended regulations, and raised their hats in token of farewell," he remembered, "to which, first casting my eyes about to see that no watchful superior was in view, I responded by bringing my musket to a 'present.'" The sides, even then so joined by brotherhood, separated with salutes, leaving in sorrow. The men of West Point had been fighting and even dueling over the question of slavery for years. The idea that they were going to start killing each other seemed absurd.

But the farther back you look, the more inevitable events appear. How could there not be a civil war after bloody Kansas, after John Brown landed at Harpers Ferry? How could there not be a civil war after slaveholding congressman Preston Brooks beat the abolitionist Senator Charles Sumner past unconsciousness with a gold-tipped cane on the floor of the Senate? How could there not be a civil war after South Carolina ignored federal tariffs during the nullification crisis of 1832? After the battles over the gag order?

In hindsight, America's policy of Manifest Destiny made the civil war impossible to avoid. As each territory opened—Missouri, Kansas, Texas—the question of whether America was a slave or free country had to be answered, and there was no answer. The opening of each new territory posed the impossible question: What is America?

Before the first civil war, nobody saw the catastrophe coming, but the moment it started, it was inevitable. Events today appear chaotic and confusing from close up, but if you look behind the fury, it's not hard to perceive their direction. Inertia and optimism are powerful forces. It's so easy to pretend it's all going to work out. It's easy to obsess over the immediate chaos, too, over what spark might engulf the whole country in sudden flames. Nobody wants what's coming, so nobody wants to see what's coming. At critical moments in history, the future stares us right in the face. We can never manage to look it in the eye.

The Preparations Already Underway

There will be those who say that the possibility of a new civil war is alarmist. All I can say is that reality has outpaced even the most alarmist predictions. Imagine going back just ten years and explaining that a Republican president would openly support the dictatorship of North Korea. No conspiracy theorist would have dared to dream it. Anyone who foresaw it foresaw it dimly. The trends were apparent; their ends were not.

Right now, elected sheriffs openly promote resistance to federal authority. Right now, militias train and arm themselves in preparation for the fall of the Republic. Right now, doctrines of a radical, unachievable, messianic freedom spread across the internet, on talk radio, on cable television, in the malls. Right now, radical Americanism craves violent resolution to its political fantasies. Right now, the faith in democracy has shattered. In the aftermath of Biden's election, a YouGov poll found that 88 percent of Republicans do not believe that Biden won legitimately.

The intelligence services of other countries are preparing dossiers on the possibilities of America's collapse. Foreign governments need to prepare for a post-democratic America, an authoritarian and hence much less stable superpower. They need to prepare for a broken America, one with many different centers of power. They need to prepare for a lost America, one so consumed by its crises that it cannot manage to conceive, much less to enact, domestic or foreign policies.

The purpose of this book is to give readers access to the same advance information. These dispatches are projections but not fantasies. The next civil war isn't science fiction anymore. The plans to the first battle have already been drawn up. And not by novelists. By colonels.

THE BATTLE OF THE BRIDGE

Until the killing starts, the uprising looks like a party. By the river, near the bridge, the anti-government patriots gather around bonfires. In their torchlit evening rallies, thick with the smoke of burning effigies and chants of "Not my president" and "America for Americans" and "This bridge stays open," the militias work themselves into livestreamed nightly frenzies, always ending with automatic weapons firing into the air. Their costumes are a mishmash, like their ideologies: Boogaloo bois in Hawaiian shirts, neo-Confederates in full array, militiamen dressed like they're about to go hunt deer. The Sheriff, as always, wears his uniform: pressed black slacks, a tan shirt, a black Stetson. He is on the scene, with his deputies, to guarantee order, but mainly he's the celebrity of the occasion, the man who has defied the government in the name of the American way of life, the freedom fighter, the rebel. Laughter curls up with the smoke of the bonfires. There's a glee in the brotherhood, glee in the spectacle.

On the perimeter across the county line, the US forces wait in silence. Their mood is somber. The general in charge of the first full-spectrum operation in the homeland* has his orders. The moment is still nauseating. The General doesn't fear the enemy.

---

* The colonel who talked me through the planning for full-spectrum operations in the homeland would only speak on the condition of anonymity due to threats. After learning of his involvement in constructing homeland scenarios, anti-government patriots took out billboards in his neighborhood with his face on them asking why he was planning an assault on his country's liberty. The FBI and, more importantly, his wife had concerns for his safety. I am grateful for his courage in speaking to me.

The rallies look more like Halloween than a movement, drawing a chaotic collection of angry and slightly ludicrous fanatics. Even the Sheriff has a faint tinge of failure around him—as if anyone knocking that black Stetson off his head would make him burst into tears. The anti-government patriots are armed with automatic weapons and IEDs and various ghost guns of their own manufacture, including hopped-up handmade rocket-propelled grenades and improvised drones. The General knows that their firepower, impressive to civilians, won't amount to much against a professional army. He has Apache helicopters and Marines.

The Army of the Interstate, as CNN has christened the anti-government patriot forces massed near the bridge, are threatening the sovereign power of the United States. Still, the General has doubts. Are they a genuine threat to the Union or just a bunch of hooligans letting off steam? Are they traitors or festivalgoers? The decision to use American soldiers to spill American blood is different from a police action. The General is about to wage war on American citizens, entitled to the freedom of expression and association and guaranteed the right to possess weapons.

And how would a bloodbath look? Sixty years of American experience has taught the same lesson about counterinsurgency: If you lose, you lose. If you win, you still lose. But the General has his orders. He has no choice but to begin the next civil war. Nobody feels he has a choice.

Right Wing Preparations for a Civil War

In the immediate aftermath of Biden's election, calls for active armed resistance against the federal government spiked. Several of the president's lawyers called for acts of violence against election officials. Michael Flynn, a retired US Army general and Trump ally, tweeted the press release from an Ohio-based conservative group calling for a "limited form of martial law." Later he would approve the idea of a Myanmar-style coup. A speaker at a rally led by Donald Trump Jr. said, "We're getting ready to start shooting." The intensity of the violent rhetoric may have been new; the message wasn't. Since 2008, American conservatives have been actively preparing for civil war. They have been preparing intellectually by predicting civil war and rehearsing its possibilities. They have been preparing materially by training themselves and gathering weapons.

It is no longer accurate to describe civil war proponents as "far right." Before 2008, only the most extreme groups on the margins of the conservative movement held secessionist beliefs. Now openness to violent rebellion against federal authority is a mainstream position. On September 12, 2016, when expert opinion stood in more or less complete consensus on the imminence of a Hillary Clinton victory, Matt Bevin, then governor of Kentucky, openly suggested violent resistance. "Somebody asked me yesterday, I did an interview, 'Do you think it's possible, if Hillary Clinton were to win the election, do you think it's possible that we'll be able to survive, that we'd ever be able to recover as a nation?'" he told a crowd at a Values Voters Summit. "And while there are people who have stood on this stage and said we would not, I would beg to differ. I do think it would be possible, but at what price? At what price? The roots of the tree of liberty are watered by what? The blood of who? The tyrants, to be sure, but who else? The patriots.

"Whose blood will be shed? It may be that of those in this room. It might be that of our children and grandchildren."

That's not some guy blasting off in a Facebook post, or a conspiracy theorist spouting dark nonsense from a random street corner. That's the governor of Kentucky, calling for bloody insurrection.

Vague predictions of the collapse of the Republic have been a mainstay of right-wing talk radio since the 1990s. Right-wing television has made calls for disunion much more specific. "This country is headed towards a civil war in terms of two sides that are just hating each other and if Robert Mueller wants, there's a big red button in the middle of the table," Sean Hannity said on Fox News on April 2, 2018. "And if Robert Mueller is so pompous and so arrogant and so power hungry and so corrupt that he's going to hit the red button, he's going to ignite a battle we've not seen in this country before."

The genre of future civil war fantasy, which is more extensive than you might imagine, is almost exclusively right-wing. The secession of Texas from the Union is a particularly rich vein. Armed conflict with the federal government is one of the most popular fantasies in the United States today. Sometimes the would-be warriors know they're pretending. In American MilSim—an extreme sport that blends historical reenactment with live-action military simulation to come as close as possible to real combat—scenarios of American insurrection make for plausible backgrounds. Many more Americans are not aware they are fantasizing. In 2015, Jade Helm 15, a routine military exercise across the southern United States, spawned a vast labyrinth of conspiracy theories. Millions believed their own government was preparing the American people for a Chinese invasion. Others believed the operation would coincide with an asteroid collision. Alex Jones claimed that "helm" was an acronym for "Homeland Eradication of Local Militants." Texas governor Greg Abbott, apparently swayed by the notion that the federal government was about to seize control of Texas by force, sent the Texas State Guard to monitor the operation. The disinformation pipeline flows into real power: internet-generated fantasies move through conservative media into the arena of policy. Fantastic visions bleed into real politics. The Texas governor responds with troops to theories with no basis in reality.

The fantasy of a civil war has established a place for itself on all levels of the American conservative system—radical groups, media personalities, elected officials. All it will take is a symbol, a hook, to catch their anger, their sense of being under threat, to focus their belief in the fantasy of cleansing violence.

The Bridge

By the time the fighting begins, no one will remember that it started over a bridge. Not an important bridge, not one of the feats of human excellence that define American achievement. Not the Brooklyn Bridge, not the Golden Gate, but a small two-lane bridge nobody bothered to name over a river ordinary people need to cross in a small rural county that loathes the federal government and has decided not to obey its mandates anymore. The bridge would make a perfect symbol for the hard right.

Nothing embodies decaying American government more completely than its bridges. Of the 616,087 bridges in America, nearly 40 percent are fifty years old or older. The United States constructed infrastructure miracles, then didn't bother to maintain them. Maintenance requires money, and nobody notices a bridge not being dangerous. The current backlog of bridge rehabilitation stands at $171 billion. In 2016, nearly 10 percent of the nation's bridges were structurally deficient. The bridge that will be the

inciting incident of the first battle of the next civil war could be
any one of them.

At this particular bridge, agents from the Federal Highway
Administration show up for a routine inspection. They find crumbling concrete, water damage from improper sealants, and thin-
ning gusset plates that could tear the line of rivets. They have no
choice but to direct the county's supervisors to close the bridge as
a danger to public safety. Repairing the bridge won't be simple,
either. The Environmental Protection Agency requires an environmental assessment before any repairs can be made. Due to funding
cuts and the backlog of infrastructure projects with mandated assessments, the EPA won't be able to give a hard deadline. Meanwhile the bridge will be barricaded with concrete stanchions and
barbed wire. Drivers will have to take the long way around.

The Sheriff will wake up one morning to find his constituents
furious. The politics won't matter, or even register, with the residents of the county. They'll just be pissed that they don't have
their bridge. When the Sheriff stops in at the local diner in town,
beside the county offices, his people will give him an earful. What
is a government for—what do you pay taxes for—if not to keep
the bridges open?

Steeped in the right-wing internet and an active member of
the Constitutional Sheriffs and Peace Officers Association, this
Sheriff decides to turn himself into a hero. In a fit of outrage and
a genuine sense of service to the community, he straddles an exca-
vator and pulls aside the concrete stanchions and barbed wire to
reopen a closed bridge. A local Fox affiliate covers the scene, and
it makes great television: the Sheriff with his laughing face as he
operates the wall clamp barrier lift that moves the concrete to one
side. That's his first crime, since he isn't licensed to operate heavy

machinery. In the interview that follows the bridge clearance, he stands stiffly, his uniform pressed and starched. He keeps his Stetson hat on.

"Why have you opened the bridge, Sheriff?" the reporter asks.

"The distinguished representatives of the Federal Highway Administration and the so-called Environmental Protection Agency do not, I am afraid, understand the needs of the people of this county, and I do."

"Do you expect any trouble from the government?"

The Sheriff smiles. "I remember that Ronald Reagan said that the nine most terrifying words in the English language are 'I'm from the government and I'm here to help.'"

"Sheriff, have you spoken with the Federal Highway Administration or the EPA?"

"I don't think I need to speak with them. I think the doctrine of interposition is well established."

"What do you say to those who say the bridge is unsafe?"

The Sheriff shrugs. "This is a free country. Anyone can choose to use the bridge or not to use the bridge. You know, my grampy always told me life is unsafe."

The "grampy" comment lifts the segment into the mainstream. The networks pick up the drama of the bridge: *The Late Show* jokes about how conservatives believe in "the God-given right to die in bridge accidents." Tucker Carlson rants for ten minutes about why the left-wing media has grown so comfortable mocking law enforcement. They bully the Sheriff, he concludes, because he's a government figure who's done something that people wanted for a change. The *Wall Street Journal* publishes an editorial entitled "A New Horatio on an Old Bridge." From the beginning, the Sheriff divides America, along the lines that already divide it.

The View from an Interpositional Sheriff Today

You do not have to imagine this defiant sheriff. You can meet a version of him right now.

To this day, Richard Mack is proud that he reopened a closed bridge when he served as the sheriff of Graham County in Arizona from 1988 to 1996. "We had a bridge out on the east side of the county and two different agencies told us we couldn't fix it," he remembers, his voice charged with cheerful contempt. "The EPA and the Army Corps of Engineers told us we couldn't fix it until they finished their environmental impact study. Well, it went on for ten, eleven months. And the county commissioners finally got the courage and they voted unanimously to fix the bridge. Then the federal government threatened to arrest the county commissioners and all the maintenance workers at the site. I got involved. I told them, 'I get along with everybody but you guys aren't arresting anybody in my county. You guys make any effort to arrest anybody in my county, I'll arrest you. You do not come in here and try to prevent us from fixing a bridge.'" Mack believes in the doctrine of interposition—"standing in the way"—the sheriff's duty to resist government abuses. "The founding fathers fought a war to oppose government abuses," he adds. In *Cooper v. Aaron* (1958), a desegregation case, the Supreme Court rejected the constitutionality of interposition, whether on a county or a state level. That clear ruling has done nothing to stop the popularity of the idea among local law enforcement.

Mack is not alone in his beliefs about the power imbued in the role of sheriff. The Constitutional Sheriffs and Peace Officers Association has about 5,000 members. They are what anti-government patriots with power look like. "The FBI has very little authority in the county," Mack argues, their role being properly limited to investigations of counterfeiting, treason, border protection, piracy, and the violation of treaties. The sheriff, for Mack, is a sacred figure imbued with a constitutional role of resistance to federal authority. "The federal government is not supposed to be big," he says. "The federal government was designed to be small and impotent." The sheriffs elected across the United States are there to ensure that impotence, he believes.

The United States has always had resistance to government in its blood. The resistance is growing louder and angrier.

The Political Consequences of Information Pollution

The next civil war will be a war over meaning. The division begins in the information systems: the media, the machinery of electoral politics, the internet, and social networks. Every study of virality since the origin of social media has shown that, after the experience of awe, moral outrage is the strongest driver of traffic. When you combine the power of outrage with the low risk of judgment from behind a screen, along with what psychologists call "the reduction of empathic distress"—the basic inhumanity that the facelessness of the internet permits—you have a very powerful machine for dehumanization, no matter what content goes into it. This phenomenon isn't limited to the United States. The same effect has been seen in Bangladesh, the Middle East, and elsewhere, with mass death as a result.

Since anger drives the information networks and the networks create meaning, it should come as no surprise that twenty-first-century sheriffs love to put on angry shows. They want to be celebrities. In 2017, Arizona lawman Joseph Arpaio ignored the federal government's injunctions barring him from "immigrant roundups," but even after he was convicted of criminal contempt of court, President Trump pardoned him. He earned his pardon by being famous. In his tent city chain gangs, large prison camps in the 1990s in which the humiliation of criminals was used as a major deterrent, he insisted that inmates wear pink underwear. He sold pink handcuffs during his promotional effort for his book tour. It's not just Arpaio, either. Trump-loving sheriff David Clarke has worn twenty-two medals during his media appearances despite never having served in the armed forces.

The information networks of the United States have become polarization machines. They work by anger, through anger, toward anger. The force of virality is indistinguishable from divisiveness. The power of spectacle is driving American politics, on the right and the left. That spectacle demands larger and larger stakes. It distorts all perspective. It turns small, minor issues—like the closure of a rural bridge—into the grandest possible questions—like the authority of the federal government.

The Spectacle of the Sheriff

Once the Sheriff becomes a celebrity, the bridge becomes a constant point of media attention.

The Sheriff speaks to Fox News earnestly on the need to rein in the federal government and the impulse to restore freedom. "This is not a country built on shutting down bridges," he says. "It's not a country built by bureaucrats. It's not a country built by men who listen to bureaucrats either." He will automatically be a hero to talk radio and cable news, appearing nightly on their shows. The Sheriff will be equally happy to speak to white nationalists and European heritage sites.

Inevitably, he becomes a meme, chopped up, parodied, pornified, set to music, idolized, demonized, worshipped, set inside pastiches of horror films or old television shows or earlier memes, yet another image to be demolished and reconstituted. To liberals he is a terrifying autocrat, an icon of the country tearing itself apart. To mainstream conservatives, he represents the dedication to small government. To the talk radio entertainment complex, he offers a mockery of the political order and a rambling carnival of ratings-grabbing turmoil. To the fringes of the hard right, he's an outright hero.

When he speaks to mainstream outlets, like the *New York Times* and the *Washington Post*, he tends to be polite and moderate, playing up his folksiness. "I just wanted to keep the people moving," he tells the *Boston Globe*. "It just seems to me like it's my job to get out of people's way."

"You're in the government's way, though."

"I suppose that's so. I can't imagine I have a great number of friends in Washington these days. But I guess I feel it's my job to get the government out of people's way, too."

With Fox News and other right-wing outlets, he's more serious, less jokey. He speaks earnestly of the need to rein in the federal government and of the impulse to restore freedom. After one of his interviewers goes on a long rant about how the government is using the EPA and other federal agencies to promote the interests of Blacks and Jews over the interests of whites, he says nothing except "I hear what you're saying." He never agrees or disagrees, which allows mainstream media to continue to treat him as more than a fringe figure.

"What will you do when the FBI comes for you?" Geraldo asks during a live segment.

"Well, sir, if the FBI came to arrest anyone in this county, they would need to consult with the sheriff."

"And you have a connection there."

"I feel like I know the sheriff pretty well, sir."

Always at ease, always in his pressed and starched uniform, always in his Stetson hat, the Sheriff is caricature and legend at once. His humility seems as bottomless as his arrogance, his strength and formality of manners balanced by the vulnerability in his eyes. The man of quiet defiance radiates the impression that the world is about to be taken away, that the last decent glint of humanity is about to be extinguished, that he alone stands in front of a tide about to swallow the world. Half the American people love it.

He becomes two memes straightaway. In the "grampy said" meme, on one side a journalist asks him a vastly complicated or insoluble question—"How do we overcome the environmental crisis while maintaining economic growth and diminishing income inequality?" or "Why does a loving and all-powerful God allow children to get cancer?"—and in the next frame the Sheriff answers: "Grampy said . . ." In the "at ease" meme, the image of the Sheriff standing at ease is posted into ever more ridiculous situations—on a mountaintop, in a 1990s porn star orgy, in a scene from the *Saw* franchise.

Slowly, militias start filtering into the Sheriff's county. They bring flags. They aren't American flags.

How to Think Through the American Hard Right

In these dispatches, I use the term "anti-government patriot" to describe the hard right in the United States. I believe the phrase captures the basic connection between a wildly diverse collection of groups. They hate the government but they love the country. The intensity of their hatred for government is how they express their love for their country. They believe that the federal authority is destroying the true America.

That core belief expresses itself in hundreds, if not thousands, of different ways. Tracking the changing beliefs of the hard right would require daily, sometimes hourly reports. Conspiracy theories are metastasizing across American conservatism continuously. Who the Boogaloo bois are now will be different by the time you are reading this. They began as a hard-right white power group; they have split into a race war wing and a libertarian wing. Some have showed up recently at Black Lives Matter protests in support of the protestors. Similarly, QAnon, a wide-ranging conspiracy theory grounded in the belief that high-level Democratic operatives have been involved in elaborate pedophile rings, has morphed into a whole range of conspiracies around the "deep state." These ideologies are fragile but oddly durable; they smash and reform all the time.

The hard right in America today ranges from men and women a few steps over from small-government conservatives to outright criminals and the insane. Their reasons for hating the government vary. There are tax protestors who believe that income tax is illegitimate and there are sovereign citizens who don't believe that the Fourteenth Amendment is valid. Differences of style matter, too. The alt-right is polished in its racism. The Ku Klux Klan isn't. There are Second Amendment absolutists and there are minutemen and there are sagebrush rebels and there are border vigilantes. Even among the white power wing of the anti-government patriot movement, there are white supremacists and there are white nationalists and there are white identitarians and there are neo-

Nazis—none of them exactly the same in motivation or in action. Many of these intellectual currents run into each other. They often overlap. But none requires the others. It is possible to hate the federal government's involvement in public lands and not be, at the same time, a white nationalist or even a racist. There are sovereign citizens who are Black.

Rather than following one coherent ideology, or series of ideologies, the hard right offers a buffet of sensibilities. Each individual picks and chooses: white power, Christian identity, the inviolability of the Second Amendment, tax loathing, the belief in the illegitimacy of the federal government. Conspiracy theories blossom, and intertwine, and separate. New factions appear every couple of months. The militias emerge from a general anti-government feeling that is the widespread base of support—at least a third of the country. That base is the ground from which domestic extremists sprout.

Don't mistake intellectual incoherence with weakness. The power of the anti-government patriots is real and rising. The hard right is much larger and much more violent than almost anybody believes. A study from the Institute for Family Studies in 2018 suggested that nearly 11 million Americans "share the attitudes" of the alt-right alone. The vast majority of terrorism in the United States comes from the hard right, and the University of Maryland's Global Terrorism Database shows the number of terrorist incidents in the United States has tripled since 2013. During the decades in which America obsessed over the rise of Islamic terrorism in the Middle East, it failed to notice the rise of a homegrown equivalent, radical Americanism, a pocket heartland ISIS.

The bipartisan Center for Strategic and International Studies concluded in 2020 that "far-right terrorism has significantly outpaced terrorism from other types of perpetrators, including from far-left networks and individuals inspired by the Islamic State and al-Qaeda. . . . Right-wing extremists perpetrated two thirds of the attacks and plots in 2019 and over 90 percent between January 1 and May 8, 2020." The success of hard-right terrorism has led to a rise in accelerationism: the desire to hasten a civil war by inciting violent chaos. Two neo-Nazi organizations, the Atomwaffen Division (using the German word for atomic weapons) and The Base, a white power version of Al Qaeda, promote terrorism as part of a plan to institute a white ethnostate after a systematic collapse of the United States.

Even the fringe movements of anti-government patriots are sizable. A low estimate of the number of sovereign citizens in the United States starts at 300,000, the number of people who refused to file their taxes out of principle, a felony. To put that in perspective, the Weather Underground was estimated, at its peak, to contain a thousand members. The estimate of the number of Black Panthers rises as high as 10,000, a highly debatable figure; the Panthers talked a great deal about the need for violence but managed to commit very little. The most power they ever gained were seats on a few local government commissions in Oakland. The Panthers and the Weather Underground caused immense panic in the late sixties—and massive responses from the FBI. The sovereign citizens, and the anti-government patriot movement as a whole, are much more numerous; they are armed, they are anxious for the government to fall, and they regularly murder dozens of people a year. In 2012 the FBI began listing sovereign citizenry as its top domestic terrorist threat.

Sovereign citizens believe they are sovereigns unto themselves and therefore do not have to pay attention to any laws that legislatures pass or to law enforcement. They believe that the federal government is a fictitious entity that is operating outside the purview of the Constitution for the purposes of holding US citizens in slavery. Their ideas hovered on the extreme fringes of American politics until the housing crisis of 2008 and the election of Barack Obama. Then they exploded. Declining financial power and the rise of multicultural iconography—the sovereign citizens are its fruit.

The anti-government patriots, and the sovereign citizens who are their most extreme members, are the most overt reflection of lost white privilege in the United States. Fueled by the loss of faith in government and the rising sense of aggrieved white diminishment, theirs is a totalizing vision of absolute individual freedom and resistance toward the state as such. "Understanding Sovereign Citizenry ideology is like trying to map a crack that develops on your windshield after a pebble hits it. It's a wild and chaotic mess," Ryan Lenz, a senior investigator for the Southern Poverty Law Center, tells me. Sometimes the spirit of disobedience expresses itself in fanatical violence, as in the case of Jerry Kane, who killed police officers at a routine traffic stop in Memphis. At other times it expresses itself as convoluted tax dodges, as in the case of the founder of the Republic for the united States of America (RuSA), James Timothy Turner, who was convicted of posting a $300 million fictitious bond in his own name. He traveled the country in 2008 and 2009 conducting seminars about elaborate systems underlying the tax code and how ordinary people could use his knowledge of the system to excuse themselves from financial obligations—or, to put it in the FBI's more familiar terms, to defraud the IRS. Turner has been sentenced to eighteen years in prison. Bruce Doucette, a sovereign "judge" who traveled the country offering a similar financial salvation, planned alternative state legislatures. He received thirty-eight years in jail.

One pet theory of the sovereign citizens is that the Fourteenth Amendment, first passed after the Civil War, is illegitimate, making the current government merely "de facto." The real government, the government the sovereign citizens recognize or imagine, is "de jure." The movement has become famous for their elaborate disruptions of court procedure. They are masters of "paper terrorism." A favorite tactic is to take out false liens on judges trying their cases, thereby forcing a recusal. "Between 2012 and 2014, there was a massive effort in the United States to make sure that county clerks, in rural areas and in metropolitan areas, knew what to look for when a sovereign came in to file something fictitious," Lenz says. They draw vast consequences from the tiniest details. My favorite example: the flags in most American courts have gold fringes, traditionally the style of the American navy. Therefore, according to some sovereign citizen theories, when you enter court and pass out of the gallery, you are entering a jurisdiction where maritime law applies. Their theory of the straw man, another convoluted idea of legal precedent, fuses conspiracy with economic salvation in a typically secretive vision of hidden powers shaping daily reality. They believe that "there is a federal account associated with you, which the federal government has invested in you, based on your future earnings," Lenz tells me. It's a secret account that citizens have access to if they know how. "There are sovereign citizens out there who believe that the US government is run by reptilian aliens," Lenz says. "Turner said he had documents that proved that the US government had made intergalactic peace treaties with alien nations." Literally, the conspiracies go beyond the surface of the earth.

"The sovereign citizens are preparing for when the government falls, not if," Lenz says. Sovereign citizens commit crimes more or less daily in the United States. In April 2014, Jerad and Amanda Miller, sovereign citizens who were present at the Bundy standoff, killed two police officers at a CiCi's Pizza in Las Vegas. They pinned a note to one of the cops' bodies: "This is the beginning of the revolution." They told the horrified onlookers: "The revolution has started." In 2014 a survey conducted with US officers in intelligence services across the country found sovereign citizens to be law enforcement's top concern.

The resistance movement to the United States is broad and deep and violent. It is intellectually incoherent but ferociously devoted. This is essential to understand: the incoherence is part of the appeal. The lack of a coherent or stable ideology means that the knowledge is esoteric, the world illuminated by a hidden meaning known only to the initiated. When you don't have an explicit ideology, a practice, you can't be blamed for the effects of that ideology: If you call yourself a Nazi, you have to embrace the history of Nazism. But with fast-moving conspiracy theories wrapped in satire, you get all the advantages of belonging to a tribe, with none of the responsibilities. The internet provides a way to flirt with reality; you can always claim you were just kidding, or you can go and kill a cop. Increasingly, accelerationism, the faction of the anti-government patriot movement that wishes to bring about civil war, is losing all ideological content. They praise the Unabomber and Timothy McVeigh alike. They just want the destruction of the state. To what purpose matters less and less.

The American hard right operates on a spectrum from the criminally insane to law enforcement officials. In a way, that spectrum makes the true size of the movement harder to perceive: you can dismiss the criminals as criminals, and the law-abiding pose no immediate threat. But the spectrum shows a breadth of support in the country at large that is not the result of local conditions. There is a widespread, if confusing, popular support for opposition to the US government. And, even more confusingly, several of those anti-government forces have moved into government. Two congresswomen elected in 2020—Marjorie Taylor Greene of Georgia and Lauren Boebert of Colorado—publicly backed the QAnon conspiracy theory. Mainstream conservatism and the Republican political establishment are both involved in anti-government patriotism. Extremist views are no longer extreme.

Confusion is a natural state at the beginning of any collapse. In other countries and in other times, it's never been clear, at least at first, whether a civil war was properly underway. Who is a rebel and who is a bandit? Who is a freedom fighter and who is a terrorist? The line between criminality and revolution blurred in Mexico, in Cuba, in Northern Ireland, in Algeria—everywhere. What if America is already in the middle of an armed uprising and we just haven't noticed? What if we're just not used to armed uprisings happening in places we know?

The Gathering at the Bridge

Neo-Confederates, white nationalists, straight Nazis, Klansmen, the alt-right, Three Percenters, Spartan youths, the American Golden Dawn, Frontiersmen, Oath Keepers—all come to the bridge brandishing swastikas, Odal runes, Black Suns, Iron Crosses, the Valknut, Confederate battle flags, Deus Vult crosses, and many other symbols. The largest militias, the ones that set up separate compounds, are the Pennsylvania Light Foot Militia, the

New York Light Foot Militia, the Virginia Minutemen Militia, and the Oregoners, but eventually militia members from all fifty states, including a lone representative from Hawaii, set up camp.

They use generators for power. They purify their water with colloidal silver. They finally have a chance to use all the materials they have bought at the prepper conferences. The area downstream of the bridge fills up with booths selling rations and weapons and tactical wear and books about manufacturing your own bazooka, and planting a garden after a nuclear event, and Muslim infiltration into the CIA, and Jewish control of the media. During the day, the space around the bridge resembles an open-air gun show.

The story dominates coverage on all formats. *Time* magazine is the first to describe them as the Army of the Interstate. CNN becomes a twenty-four-hour "Battle of the Bridge" station. Every hotel and Airbnb in the county is taken. The international press soon follows. No quantum of information is too insignificant when it comes to the Sheriff or the county in defiance. Every nuance of the arguments on all sides is rehashed on the Sunday talk shows. Meanwhile, every militant group has brought DSLR cameras alongside its arsenal and survival supplies. They livestream their resistance. The line between hard-right journalistic organizations and hard-right militias is blurry at the best of times. The crisis at the bridge erases any distinction. The struggle isn't over a bridge but over a narrative. It begins in a county but it is fought, at first, over the networks—the internet, television, the means of information.

At night, the militias gather for torchlit rallies. The most popular chant—alongside "You will not replace us" and "Blood and soil"—is "This is what democracy looks like." Every night the crowd stands on the bridge to show how much weight it can bear.

"This bridge stays open," they howl. It makes can't-miss television, wildly viral memes.

When asked by a *Times* reporter whether he supports the festival of rage in his county, the Sheriff answers, "Isn't freedom of speech wonderful?"

When Rachel Maddow describes the scene as "the Woodstock of Hate," the Sheriff approves. "I guess it's time real Americans had a party of their own." The Sheriff is an icon to the groups on the bridge, no matter their affiliation. When he speaks, he doesn't need a microphone. Everyone goes silent.

Among the swastikas and the banner of the Army of Northern Virginia, a new flag is lifted. The Black Gadsden has the traditional rattlesnake and the motto DON'T TREAD ON ME, but on a black background.

Around this time, the Sheriff begins to deputize various senior members of the larger militias. NBC coins the phrase "American ISIS" to describe the development. Fox claims the Sheriff needs deputies to maintain order during "the extraordinary surge of freedom" at the bridge. "We are officially dealing with traitors," Frank Bruni writes. Podcasters on the left predict an imminent national coup, spearheaded by the Sheriff. A ProPublica poll finds that 73 percent of Americans agree with the statement "The Sheriff represents a rebellion against the legitimate government of the United States." But only 36 percent agree that "the US government should intervene with military force."

The View from a Prepper's Conference

Again, you don't have to imagine. The anti-government patriots are preparing now for the collapse of the United States. They are readying themselves for a conflict with their own government. You can go see them.

On the fringe of Bowling Green sits Woodland Mall, where the Ohio Prepper and Survivalist Summit takes place. The several dozen booths sell not only a lot of guns but also solar-powered flashlights that keep a charge for seven years and plastic buckets containing 120 emergency rations for $274.99. (Gluten-free is available if you plan on a gluten-free collapse.) The summit offers a range of courses on the art of retreating in the event of civilizational collapse, ranging from bug-out planning and building caches and black-powder DIY to bushcraft skills and homeopathy, archery and self-defense. Frontiersmen—an organized prepper group—wander the booths with pistols at their belts. The Oath Keepers wear black shirts identifying themselves as security.

Preparations for the new collapse look exhausting. Jim Cobb is the author of several books, including *Prepper's Armed Defense*, and Cobb's plans for surviving the apocalypse are intensive. Pick three bug-out locations in different directions from your residences, all of them under 200 miles from your home so you can get there without a full tank of gas in your car. You should also plan three routes to each of your three locations. That makes nine routes in all. Don't mark them down on a map, either. What if you're stopped on the way? Then people can tell where your bug-out locations are and go steal your stuff. Cobb tells us to use our heads: "Use it for more than a hat rack." At each bug-out location, Cobb suggests keeping the weapons cache on the outskirts of the property in case of "unplanned party attendees." And above all, drill. Your wife might not like it. Your kids might not like it. "Drills suck," as Cobb says. Still, you have to drill to build up "muscle memory." Everybody needs a bug-out bag, of course. He stalks the front of the classroom with the jaunt of a middle manager explaining effective sales strategy to a regional office for the nth time.

The fantasies of the preppers are absurd and melancholy, but they aren't useless. Eve Gonzales teaches home medicine and post-collapse gardening. She has the sad eyes of a woman growing tired of explaining things to people who will not listen, like she's run the school library in a small town for too long. Beside me, a female soy farmer with gray hair and a floral shirt from the seventies talks to a guy in a National Guard T-shirt with a copy of Gary Lincoff's *The Joy of Foraging* about the merits of eating Queen Anne's lace. It's very good for you but you have to be careful. It's so similar to hemlock.

Gonzales wants her audience to develop "the skill of sprouting." Bean sprouts are full of nutrients and grow quickly. She wants us all to buy heirloom seeds, which self-germinate. You can harvest seeds from them, but you should remember that germination declines by up to 50 percent over five years. And don't forget about protecting your harvest. The preppers agree that, in a crisis, everybody wants to steal from everybody else. The biggest thief will be the government. Gonzales warns us equally about looters and the federal authorities. Her solution is brilliant: Fill your garden with nutritious weeds—dollar weed, lamb's-quarter, amaranth, dandelions. "The government, by executive order, can take everything, but they don't take dandelions," she says.

Nick Getzinger, the executive officer to the president of the Ohio Oath Keepers and the owner of the Oath Keepers Outpost, teaches the class on survival caches. The caches are built out of PVC tubes and then buried at secured sites. Mainly, Getzinger fills his PVC tube with incredibly elaborate ways of purifying water. (Everyone takes for granted that the LifeStraw, a straw-style water filter, is insufficient, although everyone recommends buying one anyway.) His methodology for water purification includes a combination of hypochlorite, colloidal silver, and charcoal. For starting a fire, he uses a Fresnel lens or wax-coated matches. He recommends a Mylar blanket for a solar oven and Vietnam-era ponchos because of the way they roll up. A complete cache also includes snares, a hacksaw blade, seeds, silica packs, and oxidizer to reduce the effects of moisture. He advocates a new kind of slingshot that flings projectiles from a circle ("more accurate than a wrist rocket"). As for ammunition, he suggests a consistent round in all the guns you own. You don't want to have a .38 pistol and .45 bullets, do you?

The preppers share a specific fantasy. It's not nuclear winter. It's not climate change. It is a world without authority in which roving bands attempt to raid your hard-won supplies, and self-sufficiency and self-defense determine survival. It's all conspicuously similar to what the American frontier looked like—or, rather, what the American frontier looks like in the movies. The students are often enjoined to "think like the pioneers." The preppers and survivalists aren't just imagining the end of America. They're imagining it beginning again.

And in that dream of rebirth is the seed of a radical politics. Apart from guns, the most popular items for sale are "Black Guns Matter" T-shirts and flags with the coiled "Don't Tread on Me" snake—the usual. There's a Spartan helmet with the letters ΜΟΛΩΝ ΛΑΒΕ underneath. ΜΟΛΩΝ ΛΑΒΕ translates to "Come and take," the defiant response of Leonidas, king of Sparta, when Xerxes, king of the Persians, demanded he surrender his weapons at the battle of Thermopylae. In this analogy, the US government is the Persians and the preppers are Spartans.

The high point of the Ohio Prepper and Survivalist Summit is the appearance of Challice Finicum Finch, whose father died in a standoff with the FBI. Twenty-six years old, with four kids, blond, skinny, she knows who the bad guys are. The bad guys are the federal government. What precisely happened to Finicum Finch's father is subject to debate. Nobody doubts that, in 2016, LaVoy Finicum was involved in a gunfight with federal agents as his group occupied the Malheur National Wildlife Refuge in Harney County, Oregon. Nobody seems to dispute that Finicum crashed his pickup into a snowbank and attempted to flee on foot. The FBI version of subsequent events is that Finicum was shot while reaching for a firearm and that while he was being arrested he shouted: "Go ahead and shoot me. You're going to have to shoot me."

The police declared his shooting justified. But one of the FBI agents, W. Joseph Astarita, was indicted on charges of lying and obstruction about who fired first. (He was later acquitted of all charges.) Challice Finicum Finch believes that her father was shot in the back three times and left overnight to die in the snow.

For her, the question of federal authority is not just a grand matter of democratic validity, nor is it a technical issue of jurisdiction. It is a matter of blood.

"We are in slavery," she announces to the audience.

Why are Americans in slavery?

"If you don't own anything, you are a slave."

And why don't Americans own anything?

"If you don't pay your property tax, you'll find out pretty soon if you own anything. You have purchased the right to rent from the government."

She asks: "Who's been fined by Obama, for not having healthcare?" A couple of hands shoot up. "You don't own your body."

How did Americans become slaves? Finicum Finch's answer is that they didn't read the Constitution. She enjoins the audience to weekly, even daily reading of their foundational text.

What did Finicum Finch find in it? She found that the states supersede the federal government because the states created the federal government. She discovered that the federal government holds "80 percent" of land in the west, land to which it is not entitled.

She tells the story of a recent encounter with the police. "I got pulled over and, like a little slave, I did everything the officer told me to do and then I get home and I realize, hey, that was wrong. He just trampled my rights."

The audience is full of veterans and police officers. The armed anti-government forces are rising among those who serve or once served the government they condemn. Finicum Finch loves the police forces and those who serve. She repeats that she isn't anti-government; she's just anti–corrupt government. That line is the line on which the new radical Americanism rides.

The men and women wandering the stalls at the Prepper Summit buy the books and the seeds and the guns to imagine themselves resisting federal authority. The books, the seeds, the classes, the guns—all of them are accessories to a story Americans tell themselves in increasing numbers. In that story, the US government is the bad guy and they are the good guys.

At the Woodland Mall they know that whatever freedom is, they don't have it. "How far are you willing to be pushed?" Challice Finicum Finch asks. "When is your faith going to be bigger than your fear?" And while it seems impossible to imagine the overthrow of the system of the American government at this moment in time, "do we not believe in a God of miracles?"

The Counterprotestors

"New freedom riders" form in the closest major city to plan opposition to the rise of the Sheriff and the gathering of the militias. "John Lewis Battalions" plan to "not cross the bridge." They paint signs with "This Is Still America" on them and "The Punishment for Treason Is Death" and "No Amerikkka."

Proud Boys meet the first group of protestors as their bus pulls into a Red Roof just across the county line. They have automatic weapons and baseball bats. The Proud Boys grab and drag the counterprotestors, beat them at gunpoint, and throw them back on the bus.

By the time the first new freedom riders arrive at a hospital, three are dead. The Sheriff shrugs off the deaths: "I think it's common sense not to go where you're not wanted."

He refuses to take any actions against the Proud Boys. "Freedom of expression and freedom of association are bedrock American values," he says.

Asked if he believes beating protestors at gunpoint is protected under the First Amendment, he smiles. "I think those boys expressed themselves rather well."

The organizers of the new freedom riders cancel their planned protests. All stations begin covering the story from the ground twenty-four hours a day. The rebellion in the county is the only story.

Digression on the Threat from the Left

The extreme left in the United States is weaker than the extreme right on every level. Nonetheless, left-wing interposition—refusal to recognize governmental authority—is real. The closest analogue to the Battle of the Bridge that I am imagining is CHAZ, the Capitol Hill Autonomous Zone, established by progressive forces in Seattle during the Black Lives Matter protests.

The autonomous zone amounted to a collection of vague sensibilities—with candlelit shrines to George Floyd, community gardens, a designated smoking area, and a "no cop co-op" where protestors could supply themselves for free. CHAZ exposed the weakness of the far left, intellectually and materially. The group published a thirty-point list of demands that went well beyond simply abolishing the police: "We *demand* a retrial of all People in Color currently serving a prison sentence for violent crime, by a jury of their peers in their community" was on the list. No mainstream political Democrat took their side.

Without the police, the community couldn't provide security for itself. Proud Boys and Patriot Prayer activists threatened the collective, and an executive order by the mayor of Seattle confirmed "an increase of 525%, 22 additional incidents, in-person-related crime in the area, to include two additional homicides, 6 additional robberies, and 16 additional aggravated assaults (to include 2 additional nonfatal shootings) between June 2nd and June 30th, 2020, compared to the same period of time in 2019." CHAZ became an accidental study of the impotence of the Left: political incoherence and no real means of defense.

Left-wing radicalism matters mostly because it creates the conditions for right-wing radicalization. "It's the interplay, the dance, between the extreme left and the extreme right that can become an escalating spiral," Ramón Spaaij tells me. He's a sociologist of violent extremism from Amsterdam who works with law enforcement agencies to determine the signs that point to the likelihood of terrorism. The action by one fringe leads to a reaction from the other, and so "they radicalize each other. It's an interactive process."

A political interposition in the United States and the subsequent political crisis is much more likely to come from the right. It's not that the left is less angry or less threatened by its opponents. Rather, the left lacks the same consciousness of resistance; they have a far less developed fantasy of interposition. Antifa does exist, but it lacks any power or the means to establish power. Left-wing defiance of federal authority, when it comes, tends to be legalistic and political, and led by state officials—the subject of the fifth dispatch of this book. In the CSIS study of 893 terrorist incidents on US soil between January 1994 and May 2020, only 22 of the 3,086 deaths due to terrorism were caused by left-wing groups.

The Political Crisis

It won't matter who the president is, or which party she belongs to, when the Sheriff takes his stand. She will need to respond. It doesn't matter how conservative she might be; to represent the federal government, she will have to defend its authority. She has no choice in the history that she makes.

The FBI is incapable of responding: a police force, designed to combat criminality, cannot serve as a military force against insurgency. The Sheriff's role has shifted from law enforcement to political resistance. But he remains an elected official and a law enforcement figure.

Also, the federal authorities aren't able to trust any law enforcement agency. They have been infiltrated by the hard right already.

The Hard-Right Infiltration of Law Enforcement

The hard right has strategically infiltrated law enforcement in the United States to such an extent that no police department or federal agency can be relied upon in a struggle against white supremacy. Connections between law enforcement and white supremacists or hard-right militias have been established in Alabama, California, Connecticut, Florida, Illinois, Louisiana, Michigan, Nebraska, Oklahoma, Oregon, Texas, Virginia, Washington, and West Virginia. These connections number in the hundreds.

Michael German, a former FBI agent who worked undercover against domestic terrorists during the 1990s, knows that the white power sympathies within police departments hamper domestic terrorism cases. "The 2015 FBI counterterrorism guide instructs FBI agents, on white supremacist cases, to not put them on the terrorist watch list as agents normally would do," he says. "Because the police could then look at the watch list and determine that they are their friends." The watch lists are among the most effective technique of counterterrorism, but the FBI cannot use them.

German has seen the infiltration of white supremacy firsthand. "When I was doing this work, I met tons of people who were hardcore Nazis. They knew the history, they had a vision for how to bring National Socialism to the United States, they published newsletters, they wrote books, they went on the speaking circuits. When they would meet me, they would say, 'Who are you here with?' And I would point to these scruffy guys in the corner, and they would say, 'Son, you gotta get away from those idiots. They're going to get you arrested. You're going to be dead to this movement. What you need to do, because you don't have any tattoos, is put on a suit and we can run you for the school board.'" The white supremacists in the United States are not a marginal force; they are inside its institutions.

Recent calls to reform or to defund the police have focused on officers' implicit bias or policing techniques. The protestors are, in a sense, too hopeful. Ordinary, everyday racism is much less a threat than activist white supremacists in positions of authority. At the protests in Oregon, law enforcement figures, from the Department of Homeland Security, from the Federal Bureau of Prisons, sometimes out of uniform, rounded up protestors. "If you look at how authoritarian regimes come into power, they tacitly authorize a group of political thugs to use violence against their political enemies," German says. "That ends up with a lot of street violence, and the general public gets upset about the street violence and says, 'Government, you have to do something about this street violence,' and the government says, 'Oh, my hands are tied, give me a broad enabling power and I will go after these thugs.' And of course once that broad power is granted, it isn't used to target the thugs. They either become a part of the official security apparatus or an auxiliary force." Neither criminals nor government forces, the camouflaged agents from the Bureau of Prisons use lawless violence with authority. They exist in a state of impunity.

Anti-government patriots have used anger against Black Lives Matter effectively to build a base of support with law enforcement. "One of the best tactics was adopting the Blue Lives Matter patch. I'm flabbergasted that police fell for that, that they actually support these groups," German says. "It would be one thing if they had uniformly decided not to target police anymore. But they haven't. They're still killing police. The police don't seem to get it, that the people you're coddling, you're taking photographs with, are the same people who elsewhere kill." The current state of American law enforcement reveals an extreme contradiction: the order it imposes is rife with the forces that provoke domestic terrorism.

The Hard-Right Infiltration of the US Military

The *Military Times* reported in a 2019 poll of 1,630 active-duty soldiers that 36 percent of active troops have seen evidence of "white supremacist and racist ideologies in the military," a significant increase since 2018, when the number was 22 percent.

The Origin of a Quagmire

At first the President hopes that the governor of whatever state the county happened to be in would ask for assistance. She could then justify intervention through the Insurrection Act: "Whenever there is an insurrection in any State against its government, the President may, upon the request of its legislature or of its governor if the legislature cannot be convened, call into Federal service such of the militia of the other States, in the number requested by that State, and use such of the armed forces, as he considers necessary to suppress the insurrection."

The Governor wants nothing to do with the request; any support for federal authority against locals would jettison his chances for reelection. So the President has to enter the county on the basis of section 333 of Title 10 US Code, which allows a president to use armed forces in the homeland to suppress insurrection or domestic violence if it "(1) so hinders the execution of the laws of that State, and of the United States within the State, that any part or class of its people is deprived of a right, privilege, immunity, or protection named in the Constitution and secured by law, and that constituted authorities of that State are unable, fail, or refuse to protect that right, privilege, or immunity, or to give that protections or (2) opposes or obstructs the execution of the laws of the United States or impedes the course of justice under those laws." She only briefly considers calling in the State Guard. It might look like the state was at war with itself.

The fifteen days the President grants for the peaceful dispersion of the militias comes and goes. The rebels continue their spectacle. They run streams of their rallies. They gleefully promote their ideologies on every available format. The President invokes precedent, the Reconstruction after the Civil War, Dwight Eisenhower calling troops into Little Rock, the LA riots. And when she calls in the military she doesn't skimp. The Attorney General and the Department of Justice serve as leads, but the US Northern Command, the Fifth Army, units at Fort Bragg and Fort Stewart, as well as the Marines at Camp Lejeune will be under the command of the General.

The General

The General comes from an old military family. He's a West Point grad, a veteran of campaigns in Iraq and Afghanistan. He is active and cheerful. He runs with his troops. He can still do eighteen pull-ups. He has a law degree from Harvard, and this, above all, qualifies him to lead the first full-spectrum operation in the homeland. At night he reads Julius Caesar in the original Latin. All of this comes out in the *GQ* profile he allows to be written about him.

The General's first priority is preventing any further militia incursions into the area. The chaos inevitable in any military campaign is vastly expanded by the novelty of a full spectrum operation in the homeland. The Sheriff is nowhere near as organized or tactically sophisticated as the Taliban or ISIS. But this time the enemy is American. The General's problems will be legal, not tactical. Killing your own people is much more involved than killing foreigners. The conquest of the county requires an army of lawyers as well as an army of soldiers.

The US Army Operating Concept defines its role as protecting "US sovereignty, territories, domestic population and critical defense infrastructure against external threats and aggression or other threats as directed by the President." So which is it? Is the army there to protect against "external threats"? Or is the category of "other threats" broad enough to include rebel militias? The General's staff shares the consensus that the terms are so vague that no action, however small, should be taken against the insurrectionists without an explicit order by the President.

The President appoints a SCRAG (senior civilian representative of the Attorney General), since the procedures in the Insurrection Act mandate that the Department of Justice be the lead agency in cases of homeland pacification. The SCRAG has been temporarily reassigned from the Department of Justice. She went to Harvard with the President.

Nobody knows, from the President to the lowest grunt, whether the conflict is a police action or the overthrow of a hostile power. And the President's public instruction to use the minimum force necessary further divides the military and the political fronts. If the conflict ends with a pile of corpses, the President will make clear to everybody that the General is the one to blame.

Two-tier authority cripples initial intelligence-gathering efforts. Executive Order 12333 from the Reagan administration explicitly decrees that the military is only allowed, in the case of US citizens, to gather enough information for situational awareness. A federal court has to authorize every individual wiretap, and while the judges work night and day, wiretaps for the residents of an entire county take time. No general, no professional soldier, will initiate combat without full situational awareness.

Intelligence gathering is hampered by the fact that the SCRAG and the Senior Federal Law Enforcement Officer fail to agree on the legal conditions for placing a name on the list of high-value targets. The staff cannot liaise with local law enforcement, since local law enforcement is the enemy. The General can't cooperate with state officials because they're security risks. No one is able to say where the loyalty of a state policeman stands when it comes to the Sheriff. Department of Defense Directive 5240.1, under "Operations Related to Civil Disturbance," states: "Upon specific prior authorization of the Secretary of Defense or his designee, information may be acquired that is essential to meet operational requirements flowing from the mission as to the Department of Defense to assist civil authorities in dealing with civil disturbances. Such authorization will only be granted when there is a distinct threat of a civil disturbance exceeding the law enforcement capabilities of State and local authorities." The SCRAG, who hasn't served in the military, interprets the phrase "essential to meet operational requirements" literally. The disagreement is more than legalistic. The insurgents need to be treated scrupulously under the Constitution. Any failure to uphold their rights justifies their claim that the government is illegitimate.

The General anticipates the legal and tactical difficulties with relative ease. He is unprepared for celebrity and its difficulties. The Sheriff turns him into a villain of illegitimacy, a Benedict Arnold, a monster of overreach. The conservative media accuses him of being under foreign influence. He sees his face distorted and his name made synonymous with the satanic. The General has to engage on the level of image manipulation, where neither he nor his staff have expertise. The struggle takes place under conditions of greater scrutiny than any US military operation in history.

Information operations are the great weakness of the American military: control over the subtle but all-powerful narratives that give governments legitimacy have always eluded even the most brilliant American soldiers. Four-star general John Galvin, back in 1986, described the military mind as "uncomfortable with warfare's societal dimension." Every general who has written a new COIN (counterinsurgency) operating manual or reported on the reasons for the failures in Afghanistan and Iraq, including Petraeus and McChrystal, have mentioned the same weakness in understanding the interplay of culture and conflict. Military leaders are, by nature, technicians rather than humanists. They are deliberately not politicians. So is it any wonder that they don't understand politics? "We've got a government in a box, ready to roll in," General McChrystal said in 2010 after the offensive into Marjah. His government in a box rolled back out less than a year later. The Joint Chiefs of Staff's failure to address the informational nature of conflict in the twenty-first century is another example of the oldest crisis in warfare. The generals are always preparing for the last war.

The MISO (military information support operations) officer is more important, the General quickly realizes, than anyone in the IPB (intelligence preparation of the battlefield) process or any of the engineering officers. His MISO officer is responsible for all show-of-force operations and media interventions during the conflict. He is also in more or less complete opposition to the SCRAG, who refuses to suspend any civil liberties pertaining to the First Amendment. After a titanic legal struggle with the Supreme Court, in the teeth of the Civil War, Lincoln was only able to suspend habeas corpus by way of a specific bill passed by Congress, and even that extreme measure required the procedural sleight of hand for which Lincoln was so famous. The nub of the problem, then as now, is inherent in facing enemies who are fellow citizens, entitled to rights.

The Sunday morning talk shows second-guess the General before he orders a single shot fired. Military experts argue that the months of delay cost the initiative, which cost lives. Legal experts argue that the proper agencies to deal with the insurrection are the FBI and the DHS, not the Northern Command. Fox News—firmly on the side of the Sheriff from the beginning—insinuates that the delay means that military command lacks confidence that American troops will fire on American citizens. The conspiracy channels churn through theories, from the General plotting with the rebels to overthrow the President to an alien presence in the county with superior technology the Fifth Army cannot defeat.

The Sheriff's defiance is electric. His daily pronouncements from the bridge sometimes attract 100 million views. Videos of the Sheriff doing push-ups, or taking off his distinctive Stetson hat to reveal his bald head, go viral instantly. Liberal Facebook is rife with elaborate comparisons of the Sheriff's career to Mussolini's and Benedict Arnold's. Kanye West appears at a Paris fashion week event wearing a Stetson. "They're afraid!" the Sheriff shouts in one of his daily appearances at the bridge. "They know they're going to take it on the chin." He alternates between supreme confidence and an apocalyptic vision of his own self-sacrifice. He is either strutting or weeping. "Not every man is born to die in his bed," he declares, his face streaming with tears. "And not every generation is going to escape the end times. We stand for freedom! Men who die for freedom!"

The Sheriff's celebrity has military consequences. Each contingent of anti-government patriots has their own media stream. They spread a vast inflammatory web of misinformation across the United States. By June, 36 percent of Americans believe that the General is a Chinese operative. A Rasmussen Reports poll finds that only 48 percent of US citizens agree with the statement "The US military should operate in the homeland during incidents of insurrection." A white nationalist in California, inspired by the resistance, firebombs the Wilshire Boulevard synagogue in Los Angeles and massacres the fleeing congregation with a legally purchased AR-15. "The federal government lit a fire," the Sheriff declares. "They think they can keep that fire here but fire is fire. You can't keep it from spreading. It's spreading all over this country." The Sheriff's popularity rises to the level where mainstream conservatives, even if they won't praise him, won't attack him, either.

The Weapons Available to the Insurgents

The insurgents, when they come, will be armed. Seventeen million Americans bought guns in 2020 alone, the largest total of any year on record. Forty percent of purchasers were new buyers.

The number of guns in the United States is somewhere north of 400 million. Americans purchase 12 billion rounds a year, and although a solid estimate of how much ammunition is in private hands is more or less impossible to ascertain, the number probably runs higher than a trillion rounds. When it comes to gun violence, the United States is a complete global outlier, beyond exceptional. There are fifty-seven times as many school shootings in the United States as the rest of the industrialized world combined. Before the outbreak of Covid-19, America experienced a mass shooting—defined as involving more than four people not including the shooter or shooters—nine out of ten days. Nearly 40,000 Americans lost their lives to guns in 2017—12 deaths per 100,000 people, compared to 0.3 in the UK and 0.9 in Germany.

There are no reliable statistics for the rise of ghost guns— manufactured at home with kits and by 3D printing—because they are unregistered, but in May 2019 the Department of Alcohol, Tobacco, Firearms and Explosives reported that 30 percent of seizures were ghost guns. Between 2018 and 2019, the number of ghost guns showing up in Los Angeles County rose by 50 percent and in Washington, DC, by 342 percent.

At this point, gun control in the United States is simply impossible.

The View from the World's Biggest Gun Show

Wanenmacher's Tulsa Arms Show in Tulsa, Oklahoma, features the ordinary American gun culture, a resistance culture, on its most expansive display. Wanenmacher's claims to be the world's largest gun show and it is certainly large enough. The event fills all eleven acres of Expo Square on the Tulsa Fairgrounds. It takes five and a half minutes, at a brisk pace, to cross from one end to the other, eight hours simply to wander through the 4,200 stalls. You could argue that the annual Shot Show in Vegas is bigger, but Shot Show invites only industry professionals, law enforcement, dealers. Ordinary Americans, not authorities, arm themselves here.

Here the guns are as varied and as beautiful as human experience itself, in every shape, color, and price point, and for every purpose. There are rifles and pistols and semiautomatics, by brand, by type, by cost. Worn old .22s you might give a kid to shoot squirrels with and .50-cals closer to cannons that look like they could take out armored cars. Long-barreled old Colts out of Westerns and neat little Glocks that possess the slick smoothness of MacBook Airs. There is cheap ammunition that you could rattle off, expensive ammunition to test your precision, materials for making your own ammunition, antique ammunition for scholars or nostalgics. Depending on your budget, you can buy an ugly little Arms Co. 22 for $69 or dream about bidding on an early nineteenth-century Artemus Wheeler revolving flintlock valued at somewhere between $100,000 and $200,000. Vendors peddle as much innovation as history: new concepts in barreling, targets, silencers, laser sights, armor, customized hearing protection, triggers that are not in violation of the ban on automatic weapons complete "with a letter from the ATF." The Barrett .50-cal with night vision and thermal scope is iconic, pure power in physical form. "He's light there. Pick him up," the dealer purrs. She's right. The weight is phenomenal, if unusually balanced in the hand, like a briefcase filled with water. The thing is a miracle of engineering, its muzzle like an arrowhead, a primitive death dealer on the edge of the future.

But it is the AR-15s that people are purchasing: you can buy one for as little as $349, you can get it custom-designed with the Stars and Stripes, you can buy it adjusted to every imaginable specification. The AR-15 is easily the most popular gun in the United States, and it's useless for hunting and useless for home defense. It's a civilian adaptation of an M16. It's been adapted for all kinds of uses with all kinds of claims about its function, but really it's for a civilian who wants to own a military-style weapon.

What moves a weapon, what really makes a gun sell, is the promise that the government is going to ban it. If the government doesn't want you to own it, you have to have it. At some gun shows, dealers post lists of weapons that are about to be banned. Any future legislation on guns—more consistent background checks, assault rifle bans—is at this point moot. The United States is saturated with weaponry. The weapons, as impressive as they are, matter less than their symbolism. The main reason Americans buy guns is to tell themselves the story of the failure of government. It's not for sport; it's not for hunting. Two-thirds of gun owners own a weapon for "protection." Protection for when the government fails them, and protection from the government. Gun culture is a culture inherently in resistance to federal authority.

Thanks to American gun culture, large groups of people proudly own weapons that the government doesn't want them to have. And that means that when the federal government faces a hard-right resistance movement, that movement will be heavily armed.

The Accessibility of Military-Grade Weapons

Many thousands of people in the United States own .50-cal rifles, and it's not that difficult to convert an AR-15 into a rough approximation of an M16. Along with hand grenades and drones, the war chest of the hard right includes radiological weapons. In two separate incidents, the first in 2008, the second in 2017, police discovered materials for dirty bombs in the residences of white supremacists on American soil. So the hard right in the United States is in possession of any and all weaponry between the pistol and low-level nuclear bombs.

The Tactical Situation

The hard right in the United States is heavily armed. It has military-grade weaponry. It has training. But the US government is better armed and better trained. Infinitely better.

The arsenal available to the American public, and to the anti-government faction of that public, is no doubt impressive. But the US Marines are the US Marines. The Marines have M16s, and M240 machine guns, and M110 sniper rifles, and they have Hummer-mounted BGM-71 TOW (tube-launched, optically tracked, wire-guided) missiles. They have Apache attack helicopters with Hellfire air-to-surface missiles.

When I asked the retired colonel about a hypothetical engagement between a hard-right militia and a professional military force, he was at a loss for an answer. Asking what would happen if a platoon of Marines faced an armed insurrection is sort of like asking what would happen if an NBA team faced the local YMCA Sunday night pickup players. It would be entirely one-sided.

There is no conceivable situation in the immediate future by which a militia force, no matter how prepared, no matter how advanced, could compete with US forces tactically.

War by Spectacle

After the months required for situational awareness, the General, following established military protocol, starts softening the town by shutting off water and power. Instead of punishing the militias, cutting utilities only hurts the remaining ordinary citizens of the county. The insurgents will have generators, satellite sticks, their own water purification systems.

The military, as usual, misjudges the informational and narrative dimensions of war. Just as they failed to understand the cultural framework of engagements in Iraq, in Afghanistan, in Vietnam, they fail again to recognize the narrative effect of the arrival of a massive US force in a small rural community. "Has the President Gone Too Far?" the *Washington Post* asks on its front page. The *New York Times* devotes an entire Saturday magazine to the legal questions opened up by an American occupation. The *National Review* argues that "even liberals are outraged by the President's overreach." The MISO officer will beg SCRAG to shut down internet access to the county, but there is no authority to do so, and the rebels remain entitled to the protections of the First Amendment.

The MISO has to use more established psyops and begin show-of-force operations. He organizes a military parade on the road to the bridge, but the insurgents, not the military, know how the symbolism works; they turn their backs. On screens across the United States, audiences watch the Fifth Army greeted by no one. For many, it's the most frightening scene since the beginning of the standoff. The President and the General begin to lose control of the story. Soldiers deployed to the county are inundated with messages from family and friends begging them not to attack "the forces of liberty."

The show-of-force operation to intimidate the Sheriff directly is more successful. Using a SEAL infiltration team, the General walks into the Sheriff's offices after incapacitating the guards. He even knocks on the office door before entering. "Hey there, Sheriff," he says, shaking the Sheriff's hand. "I just wanted you to know that I can go wherever you are without you even knowing about it."

The Sheriff is shaken but manages to smile. "I wish you'd made an appointment. I would have been happy to see you."

"You don't need an appointment when you've got the Fifth Army."

"You ever read the Constitution, General?"

What follows is a long and rather boring debate about the nature of the Third Amendment, against the billeting of militias.

The General's staff begins to make it clear to him that he has been given an impossible task. The President wants the military problem solved, and quickly. The Attorney General demands that no laws be broken. The government and the public insist the General wage war without waging war.

The rules of force issued to the Seventh Infantry during the Los Angeles riots of 1992 specified minimum levels of force in response to levels of civilian violence. The 1992 riots were inherently disorganized, with no coordinating force. But the Chairman of the Joint Chiefs of Staff issues almost identical standing rules for the Battle of the Bridge. The Chairman has to cover himself against the possibility of future prosecutions. After the battle, if the press thinks there has been too much blood, the standing rules for the use of force (SRUF) will make a perfect excuse. The General is asked to wage war on people while preserving their constitutional rights. He will, he knows, be served up as a scapegoat for the inevitable failure. On the eve of the first battle of the next civil war, the General is worried not about victory but about the paperwork.

The Immediate Cause

The conflict will obey the logic of reality television rather than revolution. The more defiant the Sheriff, the higher his engagement numbers. The most extreme opinions, the most vivid conspiracies, the most spectacular threats, gather the most attention. It will be in nobody's interest to find common cause or to explore ways out.

The mainstream media, uncovering the layers of support for the Sheriff, inevitably provides massive exposure to fringe figures with extreme positions. The camera phalanxes of pro-militia websites distribute their iconography and their message to unprecedented audiences. Virality concentrates attention. The Sheriff keeps talking about interposition and federal illegitimacy, taking ever more extreme positions. Eventually he talks himself into a declaration of independence. "When in the course of human events, it becomes necessary for one people to dissolve the political bands which have connected them with another, and to assume among the powers of the earth, the separate and equal station to which the Laws of Nature and Nature's God entitle them, a decent response to the opinions of mankind requires that they should declare the causes which impel them to the separation," the Sheriff reads out at the foot of the bridge. "And our founders, I know, would celebrate this gathering of sovereigns."

To the public, it is just another wild speech by the most famous outlaw in America. The use of the word "sovereignty" will shock the President and the General with its implication of a separate power. The protest of federal authority has morphed into a threat to national unity. The President will have no choice but to respond if she wants to preside over what are still the United States.

The Eve of the Battle

The torchlit rallies, during which the rebels whip themselves into furies, often end with weapons fired into the air. The night of the assault, a few stray bullets puncture military vehicles at the perimeter. That will be enough to justify an assault. The SRUF from the Joint Chiefs of Staff will mandate that "every incident of gunfire is to be investigated." The night before the battle, the Sheriff's forces will let off their guns as usual. This time the General will take it as justification.

The General retires to his room to pray. He knows that he will have a place in history now—the General who used American forces against American citizens. He thinks about Washington and the Whiskey Rebellion. He thinks about Lee and Grant. He thinks about Sherman marching to the sea. He cannot help remembering the sectarian conflicts of his youth, in Iraq and Afghanistan, how all their military control had spiraled out of control, how he had hated the people who had thrown him and his buddies into chaos for reasons they themselves didn't seem to fathom. The leaders he had despised asked their men to kill and to die in order to change the world. They changed the world. They had not thought through what they were changing it into. He hated the decision makers then. Now he is one. Just another confused man doing what he feels he must as history rolls over him. The General must ask other American soldiers to kill and this time their own people. Who can say what the outcome will be?

The Battle of the Bridge

Apache helicopters destroy the major points of militia communication networks within an hour. The street battle has ended by the time the media arrive at dawn. The anti-government patriots barely have a chance to resist. Those who can, flee. The rest are taken prisoner.

The group that puts up the most resistance by far is the "flipped" former members of the US military who join the anti-government patriots. A SEAL team takes the Sheriff in his office. As he is dragged away, the Sheriff shouts to a white nationalist journalist he has been streaming with: "Tell my story! If the British had captured George Washington, he would have found himself in the same position I find myself in now." Leaning back over his shoulder, he howls, "Is not what binds America together our pursuit of freedom?"

The Meaning of the Battle of the Bridge

The morning will be a harvest of ashes. Bodies litter the banks of the river. Panoramas of the bridge and the town reveal shattered corpses and craters, a quiet rural town turned into the kind of battleground scene remembered from military adventures in the Middle East. A photo captures a severed hand in the street. An orphaned child wails in a whirl of dust. The army loads bulk groups of prisoners into buses for processing in a small POW camp in the neighboring county, under the watch of cameras at a distance. CNN mourns the death of a unified country. Fox News mourns the death of liberty. Factual descriptions of the battle are indistinguishable from the conspiracy theories that light up the internet with fantasies of imminent white genocide, Chinese infiltration of the Fifth Army, Jewish cabals, the nefarious influence of the CIA and other governmental agencies, alien invasions, stories of angels coming to the aid of the Sheriff, strange beams of light illuminating the battle. The horror overwhelms; the hunger for revenge grows with what it feeds on. The slaughter bolsters the righteousness. There is no collective mourning, only panicked preparations and fury.

The battle itself matters much less than how it resonates. It sows trauma and loathing; each side regards the other as murderous traitors, the very opposite of America.

The Immediate Aftermath

The Department of Justice charges the Sheriff with treason and a few of his closest conspirators with sedition. The rest receive fines or smaller prison terms on the basis of the Insurrection Act.

All are banned from running for public office. The Sheriff, converted instantly into a martyr by the hard right, is imprisoned in the same Colorado cell block where Ramzi Yousef, architect of the first World Trade Center bombing, is serving a life sentence. The only other prisoner in that wing is the Unabomber, Ted Kaczynski. They share their hour of yard time together every day.

The Enduring Aftermath

The army could not take up residence in specific structures in the county—a violation of the Third Amendment—but they are permitted onto any property to reconnoiter. The local residents feel the intrusions, and the subtle intricacies of the supposed constitutionality won't make them feel any better.

At present, the official US counterinsurgency strategy remains a version of General Petraeus's 2006 Clear, Hold, and Build strategy. In the current edition of *Joint Publication 3-24*, it is outlined as "Shape, Clear, Hold, Build, Transition," part of a suite of counterinsurgency strategies that include the generational approach (engaging with youth who are most likely to join insurgencies) and network engagement (through social media). All of these strategies smack of desperation in their operating modes. The military holds on to these strategies because at least they are strategies, not because they work. For fifty years the US military has been defined by its ineffectiveness against insurgencies in foreign countries. Why would they do any better at home?

The problems US forces face in the occupation of foreign soil would be that much greater in an occupation of the homeland. The theory of Clear, Hold, and Build predicts that peace and security will spread like an ink stain from a central position to an entire zone of control. American troops in Afghanistan had another metaphor for the strategy: "mowing the grass"—the moment they thought they could start building, they had to begin again with the process of clearing.

The county is only a locus of a general American chaos. The insurgents rally there, then disperse. Their support moves online, or underground, everywhere. It is tactically impossible to contain a terrorist force when it is supported by broad swaths of the population outside the zone of control. Then there is the question of America's sheer size: How do you clear and hold the whole of the United States? (This question is addressed in Dispatch Four.)

The larger problem is that it is impossible to build legitimacy as an occupier: the process of holding, even with the best of intentions, is humiliating and disruptive. Anyone who has passed an American checkpoint, or entered an American prison, or even crossed the American border, knows the inherent dehumanization of the protocol. The illegitimacy of any occupying force—the French in Algeria and Indochina, the Russians in Afghanistan, the English everywhere—would meet greater opposition than ever in an American-on-American context. The defiance begins in a claim to the illegitimacy of federal authority. If you are occupying an anti-government patriot stronghold, any state-building of any kind will be forced. The locals don't want government. That's the point. But how could any force address the "drivers of violence" without the machinery of legitimization?

You don't have to look very far to find an example of a failed occupation on American soil. The South under Reconstruction spawned the Ku Klux Klan, Red Shirts, and White League—terrorist organizations that beleaguered the Northern administration until they abandoned the project of reconciliation. The resentment of the occupation after the first civil war survives to this day. The South has not forgotten the abuses of Sherman's March to the Sea. Nor have they forgiven the Northern authorities for the humiliation of subjugation. The occupied Americans hated the occupying Americans. That hatred endures.

The Rebuilding

The General resigns six months into the occupation after a scandal over the destruction of the information gathered for situational awareness. That destruction, ninety days after the battle, is mandated under Field Manual 3-28, Civil Supports Operations, but the SCRAG didn't give prior authorization. It looks like a cover-up. The General has to go.

Within six months, Americans are equally divided on the occupation. While 49 percent of respondents accept the description of the Sheriff as a traitor, 49 percent accept the description of the Sheriff as a patriot. The next civil war won't be divided between organized sides, distinct ideologies, or ethnicities. It will be a struggle between the forces of order and chaos—a struggle to preserve a coherent definition of America itself.

As part of the rebuilding effort, US forces raise a new bridge across the river.

PORTRAIT OF AN ASSASSINATION

The Assassin will be a young man, probably but not necessarily white. He could look like anyone, but it's not hard to imagine his face. Like Patrick Crusius, who shot and killed twenty-three Mexican Americans in an El Paso Walmart after posting a "white replacement" manifesto, or Jared Lee Loughner, who shot Arizona representative Gabby Giffords in Tucson in 2011, or Dylann Roof, who massacred nine congregants in the Emanuel African Methodist Episcopal Church, including state senator Clementa Pinckney, he will have that vague misery in his eyes, scraggly, unkempt, not quite grown. The three military veterans who met on a Boogaloo Facebook group in 2020 and planned to spark an uprising to overthrow the US government by means of spectacular explosions had that same look. The Assassin will be one of the many troubled young men in America. No one will expect him to assassinate the President. No one will be surprised when he does.

Stochastic Terrorism

We live in an age of what scholars call stochastic terrorism, otherwise known as "lone-wolf terrorism," although that phrase is imprecise. "Lone wolf" sounds like something from the movies. It implies that acts of spectacular violence are the result of organization, that there are masterminds hiding, like Bond villains, in distant countries, elaborating schemes and then disseminating them over networks, to be undertaken by their secretive minions. The reality of the current threat is much more banal. The background hum of hyper-partisanship, the rage and loathing of everyday American politics, generates a widespread tolerance for violence. Eventually somebody acts on it. The likelihood of a foreign government or terrorist organization killing the President of the United States is negligible. The Secret Service is simply too competent. But stochastic terrorism is a matter of an indistinct loathing, of which America has plenty. The general climate of anger and recrimination condenses into murder.

Ramón Spaaij is a sociologist of political extremism specializing in stochastic terrorism. The atmosphere of violent political hatred that permeates American society frightens him. "The background of partisan politics clearly has an influence" on shaping radical acts of political violence, Spaaij says. "If you expose many people to radical partisan politics, some of them will go on to translate that into violent action." The violent rhetoric serves as a guidance mechanism, even when it offers no explicit plan or even specific targets. "It's not a direct causal link but a number of cultural scripts that can then be drawn on," Spaaij says.

The cultural scripts of political violence are spreading across the United States and becoming more entrenched. At this moment, agents and assassins throughout America are chasing and evading one another. They are fields of force, the assassins pushing from the chaos of the rage and loathing overwhelming American politics, and the agents attempting, against that rage and loathing, to preserve the integrity of American institutions. On the agents' side is technical proficiency, an elaborate system with a "zero fail mission" mentality, and a corps dedicated literally to death. The agents have their brilliance and their courage. The Assassin has the sheer number of others like him, and time and chance.

The Tradition of Presidential Assassination

The preferred form of political violence in the United States, by far, is presidential assassination. The country has seen one civil war and no coups d'état. But assassination? The odds of being assassinated while president is one in eleven. A further seventeen presidents survived attempts on their lives. That's a lot.

Compare it to other countries: The only British prime minister to be assassinated was Spencer Perceval, in 1812. There have been two assassination attempts in Australian history, one in Canadian history. The second most lethal job in the United States, after serving as president, is industrial fishing. One in a thousand die at that job. The mortality rate of troops in combat is 82 per 100,000. So it's no surprise that the US Secret Service currently spends a million dollars a day to keep the president alive. In the United States, assassination amounts to a dimension of the political process.

The reason for the high murder rate of US presidents is that they are living symbols of national unity that no other country possesses—icons as executives. In 1782, the Founding Fathers made their motto *e pluribus unum,* a phrase with many different meanings—"out of many states, one country," "out of many peoples, one people"—but the specific role of the presidency, a leader who emerged from the general populace rather than the aristocracy, was also a key significance: "out of many citizens, one president." If you shoot the queen of England, you're not making a statement on the government of the country. If you shoot the prime minister of Great Britain, you've killed only the first advisor to the queen. The US president has an aura that no public servant or monarch possesses or can possess. When you murder a president, you murder an America that should have been.

One of the retired Secret Service agents I spoke to, a man who has thought a great deal about the motivations of the people who want to kill the president, offered me a simple explanation for the popularity of presidential assassination in the United States: "It's the fastest way to change history." When the political system cannot bring historical change, a gun will.

The Latest Trends in Assassination

The Secret Service looks into every direct and indirect threat against the president, assessing for intent, means, and opportunity. An anonymous Secret Service agent—they must remain anonymous to discuss any aspect of their protocol—described to me the extreme transformation in the assessment process over the past decade due to the proliferation of political hatred. "Years ago, it was relatively straightforward, because threats were coming in to the president via telephone calls or letters, or they would show up at the White House," he says. "Nowadays, the digital platform has allowed for threats to be made at a significantly greater volume with greater frequency by people who can remain anonymous." It is simple enough for anyone—an assassin, a kid, just an idiot—to go into any random Starbucks in America, post a death threat anonymously on public Wi-Fi, and leave. At volume, such threats are basically untraceable. The Secret Service uses artificial intelligence to deal with the bulk of violent communication, but the effectiveness of that methodology remains unproven. The only way to know if it works is if it fails. And it hasn't failed. Yet.

Counterterrorism agencies are increasingly turning to researchers like Spaaij to distinguish signal from noise. He's a sociologist of political extremism but his work is psychological. He establishes the patterns that tend to manifest themselves in individuals before they commit acts of spectacular violence. Many angry people live in America but not that many are actually preparing to assassinate political leaders. Spaaij and the Secret Service face the same problem. How do cultural scripts tip over into violent action? How does a person go from raging behind the screens to pulling a trigger?

Spaaij sees what others do not in the world of deep confusion and indecipherable rage. "If there is a common thread, it is a search for belonging, a desire for transcendence," Spaaij tells me. The state of mind that leads to assassination is both personal, "a crisis of attachment to others," and political, a crisis of history. Grandiosity plus grievance is the toxic mixture. The Assassin feels strongly that he has not received what he deserves, "seeing himself as a historical character."

"A Crisis of Attachment to Others"

The Assassin is alone but there are many like him. He belongs to a generation of lost young men, alienated misfits in a state of despair, who will do worse than their parents, who will live shorter lives than them, who will experience America as a country in decline. Like Crusius and Loughner and Roof, the Assassin is a product of divorce. His father moved away when he was a boy. His mother works long hours to support them.

He managed to graduate from high school despite a record of incidents, fits of rage that came out of nowhere, sudden viciousness against a female teacher that got him suspended. The other students tended to avoid him. History was his favorite subject but he never believed what they taught him. He was always on the web for alternate histories, cool stuff like how aliens had built the pyramids and the Nazca Lines in South America, how powerful hidden forces had shaped the world. What he really likes is the dark web. There you can see what people don't want you to see. That's what's worth reading. Plus, it's hilarious.

He didn't attend his graduation ceremony. They didn't want him, so he didn't want them.

The Assassin lives in his childhood bedroom on the top floor of his mother's house. His walls are covered in posters—a platoon of old B-52 bombers, *Reservoir Dogs*, *Moonrise Kingdom*, the scene from *A Clockwork Orange* with Alex's eyes held open. He has an old typewriter and a half-solved Rubik's cube on a small desk, alongside a broken board from his Tae Kwon Do lessons when he was a kid and some old junior soccer participation medals. He keeps a pair of binoculars on his desk. From the window he can see, over the soundproofing barriers, the interstate highway.

In the fall after graduation, his mother sits him down for a serious chat. She begins by telling him how much she loves him and how both she and his father want the best for him. She says that she knows he had a hard time in high school and that she doesn't blame him for that. The Assassin just sits and listens. The less he says, he knows, the shorter the conversations are. "You can live here but only if you find a job or go to school," his mother tells him. That seems fair enough.

He tells his mother that he's going to apply to the local community college to study carpentry, but he delays sending off the application and ends up missing the deadline. He doesn't tell his mother. She doesn't ask.

One of his father's old friends owns a hardware store. The Assassin starts to work there part-time. He likes the smell of wood. He loathes the smell of people. One day, in the lumberyard, he sees the owner laughing with a contractor, a Black contractor. He has never seen anything like it. The scene, for reasons he does not understand, fills him with a wild disgust and fear, and he just walks out and never comes back.

He wanders across the highways, past the sprawling homeless encampments, down to the local library, where he can read things on their computers he wouldn't read at home.

He types in "Why do Blacks and Mexicans hate white people so much?" The message board fills up with links.

—Because there at war with white folks. Look around.
They want jobs just for being themselves! No white man
gets that!
—The "lower forms of life" hate us because we're better.
They hate that white people built the world and they just
live in it. And it doesn't matter how much we give, they
always take more.
—Everybody just wants to be with their own. Look
around, snowflake.
—It's a war, man. It's a war.

"Seeing Himself as a Historical Character"

In the detritus and confusion of his young life, the Assassin will know one thing for sure. He will know that he was meant for more than living with his mother, with no job and no girlfriend and no friends and no prospects; that he is worth something to the world.

Political Murder as a Search for Redemption

"The political ideology becomes an excuse, an overlay, a way of giving sense and meaning to petty personal experience," Spaaij says. The violent solution becomes "a search for redemption." This is what Secret Service agents call "nefarious intent."

The résumé of Jared Loughner, who shot Arizona congressperson Gabby Giffords, is typical: dropped out of college after a series of violent outbursts; was denied entry to the military; couldn't find a job; compensated for his own degradation by way of online political forums; posted his own violent fantasies on social media and YouTube. The Assassin, wherever he might be, is stewing in his failure and idealism. He's a loser, a dreamer, a man-boy denied a destiny who feels a destiny is owed to him. His sense of his own importance only rises with each personal failure.

The search for redemption can take many forms: a petty criminal who goes into the penal system and comes out a radical Muslim; a father who defaults on his mortgage and turns to sovereign citizenship; a youth with mental health issues who can't find employment and turns to white power. The internet will blur the Assassin's soul further through "selective consumption of online materials"— carving the world into good and evil, confirming what he already knows, allowing him to produce hatred, to share hatred, to suffuse his own failures in ideology, driving him toward a single conclusion, a response to the disasters in his own life and in the country's.

"From the best of our knowledge, online radicalization starts with social alienation, which is why you see radicals from all socioeconomic classes," Alex Newhouse, lead researcher at the Middlebury Institute's Center on Extremism, Terrorism, and Counterterrorism, tells me. "Social alienation comes with anger at their lot in life. It always starts with some kind of grievance, and the contrarian viewpoint will often provide an explanation, a very clean, very convenient explanation for why they are feeling that way."

The first step in online radicalization is often nothing more harmful than basic contrarian media—the Dave Rubins or Joe Rogans of the world, shows with massive audiences, the vast majority of which never even consider violence. Contrarianism feeds on itself. "The hunger for justification for the anger that they're feeling pushes them farther and farther to fringe figures," Newhouse says. Those who become radicalized progress from ordinary, healthy alternative media to accelerationist promotion of mass murder. "The other pathway is algorithmic," Newhouse says. "Facebook, YouTube, to a lesser extent Twitter, have recommendations that actively promote engagement with increasingly fringe content." If you go into a libertarian gun rights Facebook page, on the recommendation page you find "outright civil war groups, explicitly calling for violence against the state." One thing leads to another. The system is designed that way.

What underlies the motivation to violence is a drive to understand the sense of grievance they're feeling. The despair of the Assassin's own life finds a mirror in the general despair: "There are no democratic means anymore and so violence is the only solution," Spaaij says. The Assassin sees his life falling apart before it even begins, and he sees his country falling apart before he can belong to it.

"Selective Consumption of Online Materials"

After graduation, the Assassin spends more time online. Mostly he's alone in the house. Sometimes he pretends he's going to look for work but then he heads to the library to read his favorite message boards about politics and history. The drift of his life punctuates itself with electronic dreams of grandeur and pornography and violent fantasies.

He reads mostly funny stuff, like what are the best tortures in history (the Blood Eagle) and what is the weirdest porn (the lemon party). He learns that moss grows on the north sides of trees. He learns that Napoleon liked his girlfriend not to wash when they had sex. He learns that Washington is run by pedophiles. It's well established. The press has known about it for ten years. The president organizes parties where her friends rape and murder little kids in restaurants in DC. It disgusts him.

—It's the beginning you know? You can only become a "leader" in "government" if you have no morality. It's like a test. It's a test for them to see if they're willing to rape children. Tom fucking Hanks is going to run for office. You mark my words.
—The Great Awakening. Not the Great Awokening. And all these little bitches whining about random bullshit snowflake nonsense. They don't care about CHILDREN BEING RAPED.
—You hear of a pedophile stopping at pedophilia. What's "next"? It's the thrill of the new that gets them off. It's hopeless little children today. What's the next outrage?
—We gotta fuck someone up.

There is a war going on, or there is a war about to begin. The Assassin doesn't need special inside information for that. The regular news tells him that. And it's all this bitch the President's fault. She is overseeing the annihilation of white people and men, and white people and men are finally fighting back.

It makes sense. How did the world get so fucked-up? The people with money, the people with power fucked it up.

He sees a banner ad for a gun show in town. "Sport and Hunting Equipment, Plus Historical Memorabilia!" So he goes, with $50 he's taken from his mother's purse, even though it's at a mall he hasn't heard of. The trip takes three buses; he arrives at an industrial park next to an Amazon delivery center. Inside, there is an Oath Keeper recruitment drive and a few dozen displays on folding tables. The historical memorabilia is just one booth, manned by a big-bellied old-timer who barely looks up from his work of restoring an old pistol. Under glass the Assassin sees tiny silver cups that belonged to Hermann Göring, Vietnam patches, slave shackles and bills of sale.

The Assassin peruses some of the cheaper guns, and a guy in a T-shirt that says I SUPPORT SINGLE MOMS with the silhouette of a stripper on it tells him, "I can get you that gun cheaper. That gun right there." It's a small black Ruger in the case, 9mm. "I can get you that gun right there for eighty bucks." The Assassin digs in his pocket and comes out with the $50 bill. The man in the T-shirt looks pissed off but grabs the bill and hands over a small black pistol.

The Assassin comes home and unscrews a vent in the air ducts and puts the gun inside. The Assassin has taken possession of a great gift. Everything will be all right in the end. He holds a secret.

He does one good thing that year, one thing he's proud of. A woman who claimed her daughter was killed during one of the mass shootings in California turned out to be an actor planted by people who want to take guns away from ordinary citizens, probably to make them less trouble when the government decides to impose martial law. The /freedomcosts message board he follows doxxed her and he called her number from the pay phone at the library and told her answering machine she was a lying fake bitch and she was going to get what was coming to her. The call thrilled him. He put down the receiver, radiating with excitement. He had reached out.

Later that night he posted:

—I did it. I told that fucking bitch that she could go and die.

The messages came back in a flurry:

—Fucking A!
—Every day more like us are joining in, and you should know yer not alone. And we're coming for them. We're coming for them.
—Do more little boy. You think yer fucking yackety-yak matters one whit. Action! What we need is action!

The Assassin reads later that the actress pretending to be the mother of a shooting victim killed herself. One less lying bitch with power. He may not have a job. He may not have a life. But he helped the fight.

The Assassin makes some changes to his room. He puts up a bright red 1945 poster that reads *Blitzkrieg!* and a meme of Daffy Duck with the phrase "Of course you realize this means war!" underneath.

The Assassin as Symptom

In stochastic terrorism, political murder does not emerge out of the concrete plans of ideological opponents. It's not some *Day of the Jackal*–style event. A climate of loathing finds expression in a single person with an opportunity.

The hatred motivating the Assassin will not be extraordinary. Quite the opposite. Hatred drives politics in the United States more than any other consideration. The same helplessness that motivates the assassin drives the new contemptuous politics of the United States. If you're an American conservative, you already know that open discussions of murdering political rivals are standard. If you're an American liberal, ask yourself how upset you would have been if Donald Trump had been assassinated.

As lousy and vicious and stupid as American politics might look on the surface, underneath the reality is even worse. Steven Webster is a scholar of the new breed of hyper-partisanship that is tearing the United States apart. For many years, he worked with Alan Abramowitz on the political modeling of partisan opposition in US politics, and together they published the 2015 essay "The Rise of Negative Partisanship and the Nationalization of U.S. Elections in the 21st Century," which predicted the current political lunacy better than any other. Abramowitz is a rare case of a scholar being incorrectly humble: he refused to believe the results of his own model when it predicted a Trump victory, even though it had correctly predicted every presidential election since 1992. "The model is based on the assumption that the parties are going to nominate mainstream candidates who will be able to unite the party, and that the outcome will be similar to a generic vote, a generic presidential vote for a generic Democrat versus a generic Republican," he told Vox in 2016.

Webster sees a terrible spiraling effect in action in the United States, a force that, once started, cannot be stopped except by disaster: "Partisans in the electorate don't like each other. That encourages political elites to bicker with one another. People in the electorate observe that. And that encourages them to bicker with one another." The past thirty years have led to "ideological sorting," which means that the overlap between conservative Democrats and moderate Republicans has more or less disappeared. But it's the people in the parties, not just the ideas in the parties, that have changed. Identity politics is not some phrase but a real phenomenon. The political parties, and the various branches within the political parties, have become identities by which individuals define themselves.

"There's a really big racial divide between the two parties," Webster says. "The non-white share of the American electorate has been increasing tremendously over the last few decades. And with this rise in the non-white share of the electorate, most of the non-white voters have chosen to affiliate with the Democratic Party." Not only has the Republican Party become whiter and the Democratic Party become more multicultural, the white people on each side have also changed. During the Reagan-Bush years, there really wasn't that much of a difference between the racial attitudes of white people in both parties. Over the past three decades, the Republican Party has become the party of racial resentment, "the moral feeling that Blacks violate such traditional American values as individualism and self-reliance," Webster says. "During the Obama era, 66 percent of white Republicans scored high on the racial resentment scale. For white Democrats it was around 32 percent." White Republicans have become more intolerant about the country's growing diversity. White Democrats haven't. That's the big change.

The Lack of Independents

America is becoming two Americas, Americas that hate each other, that don't speak to each other. No one occupies the middle ground anymore; everyone has separated into one side or the other, one party or the other, no matter what they may claim. "A lot of people say, 'What would happen if there was a very independent-minded candidate, a third-party candidate with no partisan label, who would come and unite America?'" Webster asks rhetorically. "That is absolutely not going to happen." In surveys, independents seem like a high percentage of Americans, but if you press those self-identified independents on their actual voting behavior, they behave just like strong partisans. Only 7 percent of Americans are truly independent in the sense that they might consider voting for a party they don't typically vote for.

The Depth of the Hatred

How to grasp the scale of the political hatred overtaking America? Thanksgiving is one way. In the aftermath of the 2016 election, economists at Washington State University found that cell phone data and precinct-level election results revealed a chilling difference between celebrations attended by opposing-party families and celebrations attended by same-party families: "Thanksgiving dinners attended by residents from opposing-party precincts were 30 to 50 minutes shorter than same-party dinners." The symbolism couldn't be more apt. Because of politics, because of the brutality of the new breed of hyper-partisan loathing, ordinary Americans can no longer enjoy their feast of plenty. They can no longer celebrate the sheer good fortune of being Americans. The report calculates exactly how much goodwill has been lost: "Nationwide, 34 million hours of cross-partisan Thanksgiving dinner discourse was lost in 2016 to partisan effects." Americans diminished the time they spent talking across party lines at the exact moment they most needed to spend more time talking across party lines.

According to Pew Research, 58 percent of Republicans view

Democrats "very unfavorably," up from 21 percent in 1994, and 55 percent of Democrats view Republicans "very unfavorably," up from 17 percent in 1994. There are 41 percent of Democrats and 45 percent of Republicans who now believe the opposing party is "a threat to the nation's well-being." But even those numbers fail to capture the emotional depth of the hatred between Republicans and Democrats. In 1960, 5 percent of Republicans and 4 percent of Democrats said they wouldn't want their children to marry a member of the other party. By 2010, it was half of Republicans and a third of Democrats. Differences of opinion have hardened into a siege mentality on both sides, leaving behind questions of policy or effective leadership. The dominant question of American political life isn't what you stand for but what you stand against.

Hyper-partisanship is now the defining hatred of the United States, and it affects so much more than how people vote or how they think about their fellow citizens' political choices. A 2015 study of polarization from the *American Journal of Political Science* found that "partisans discriminate against opposing partisans, doing so to a degree that exceeds discrimination based on race." Tribalism is no longer a mere metaphor. Democrats and Republicans really do act as tribes, with codes of purity for themselves and loathing for outsiders. This tribalism affects society as a whole. It has infiltrated commerce and religion as much as the institutions of law and government. It's worth noting that all of these trends predate Trump, sometimes by decades.

Demographic Change and Civil War

Scott Gates is an American who lives in Norway, where he studies conflict patterns at PRIO, the Peace Research Institute Oslo. His work, naturally, has been devoted to the study of political struggles in the developing world, where most civil wars take place. He is as shocked as anybody to find that his research suddenly has applications at home. The question for the United States, as it is for every other country nearing the precipice, is how strong civil society is and how much that civil society can hold back the ferocious violence of its politics. When it comes to the United States, Gates has little confidence in either point anymore.

Americans' spiral into loathing is far from unique. It's typical. A recent study from Anirban Mitra and Debraj Ray, two English economists, examined the motivations underlying Hindu-Muslim violence in India and found that "an increase in per capita Muslim expenditures generates a large and significant increase in future religious conflict. An increase in Hindu expenditures has a negative or no effect." Hindus are the dominant group in India and Muslims a comparatively poor minority. Riots start at the times and in the places in which the Muslims are gaining the most relative to the status of the dominant Hindus. Violence protects their status in a context of declining privilege. The more an underclass peacefully approaches economic and political equality, the more violent and resentful the overclass grows.

"A very similar pattern can be seen in the US right now," Gates tells me. "Over the past twenty years the white working class community, in absolute terms, gets less now than it did in the 1980s. Systematically they see their position in life getting worse. And they see their children not doing better. At the same time, the Latino community and the Black community have been improving their status relative to where they were." To be clear, white Americans don't resent growing poorer. They resent losing their comparative superiority to non-white Americans.

The revolutionary prophets of the nineteenth century, like Karl Marx, believed that the oppressed would rise up against their oppressors. In the twenty-first century, the oppressors revolt. By no means is this violent reaction against lost privilege unique to white Americans. It underlies conflicts all over the world. As privilege declines, violence increases. The Republican Party has become a white party defined by racial resentment. Declining privilege in the context of racial resentment leads historically to violence. The US Census recently announced that the country will be minority-white by 2045.

One reason why Democrats view Republicans as other and Republicans view Democrats as other is that they *are* other. The Democrats represent a multicultural country grounded in liberal democracy. The Republicans represent a white country grounded in the sanctity of property. America cannot operate as both at once. The political system quite simply cannot manage the instability of the demographic change.

The Incipient Legitimacy Crisis

According to a University of Virginia analysis of census projections, by 2040, 30 percent of the population will control 68 percent of the Senate. Eight states will contain half the population. The Senate malapportionment gives advantages overwhelmingly to white, non–college-educated voters. The 2016 electoral college results were the same as in 2020, with 232 electoral college votes for the loser and 306 for the winner. But Donald Trump lost the popular vote by 2.1 percent in 2016 and Biden won the popular vote by 3.4 percent in 2020. Even in 2020, the Democrat could have won the popular vote by as much as 6 points and still have lost the election. In the near future, a Democratic candidate could win the popular vote by many millions of votes and still lose. The federal system no longer represents the will of the American people.

The Meaning of the President

The hyper-partisan environment means that any American president will be a symbol loaded with a double meaning. She will be an icon of American leadership for half the country and an icon of oppression and illegitimacy for the other half. Symbolism matters. Countries live and die by symbols. No American president of either party, now and for the foreseeable future, can be an icon of unity, only of division.

The First Stage in the Transition to Assassination

The transition from ordinary rage-fueled American to assassin can progress gradually or overnight. "It varies from years to even days," Ramón Spaaij says. "The police would say it almost seems to happen in the moment, so how can we ever prevent this, since the person wasn't on our radar?" The Assassin will be one of millions wallowing in the sewers of loathing. He will live behind a screen, breathing in the fumes of hatred, occupying a dark corner in a country that has many dark corners. Guys like the Assassin are common enough. The vast majority do nothing.

What separates people who act from people who don't? The transition moves through three stages, or "dimensions of clusters," according to Spaaij. The first is a sudden exposure to means and opportunity, "capable of recalibrating perceived chances of success."

Sudden Exposure to Means and Opportunity

The Assassin will hear about it on the radio: the President is coming to town. She has announced a listening tour and one of the stops is going to be at that fucking high school where those bitch teachers and their student pets hated him. "The time has come to heal this great country," the Assassin hears the President saying. "And the only way we can heal is when we listen to everybody and everybody feels heard." To the Assassin her visit feels like more than a stroke of luck. The strange man sold him a gun for what he had. Now the President's coming. It feels like destiny. But he must keep it a secret.

The Preparations of the Secret Service

The Secret Service knows that the Assassin is out there. They don't know his name. They don't know who he is. But they know he is out there.

Any assassin who kills a sitting US president will have to be very lucky, and he won't succeed merely through planning. "The process the Secret Service goes through is comprehensive and proactive," my anonymous agent tells me. "What they do is they go out and proactively do an advance, they understand the threat environment, they identify, during that advance process, every threat they can think of, and they mitigate it." Location doesn't matter to the Secret Service. Preparation overcomes accident. If you're prepared, the streets of Baghdad pose no more danger than the streets of New York. "Control can come in many forms. I build control. I force control." The President's tour will require a constant application of control.

The Secret Service doesn't particularly care about the quality of the weapon available to the Assassin. A .50-cal Barrett is only useful to somebody who can find the opportunity to use it—and the Secret Service excels at denying the opportunity. In almost every real situation of danger, a pistol would be just as adequate.

The Second Stage of the Assassin's Transition

The second dimension that leads from general hate to political murder, according to Spaaij, is that "the costs associated with action are lowered and the costs associated with inaction are raised." The political and the personal fuse: the Assassin recognizes that his life no longer holds any meaningful future, so he has very little to lose.

"The Costs Associated with Action Are Lowered"

His mother brings him out of his room for another talk. "This has got to end," she says, her eyes wet with tears, the exhaustion plumb on her face. By now he's mastered tuning his mother out but he gets the gist of what follows. His mother wants him to move to San Jose to live with his father for a while. His father owns a sports equipment store where he can work and will pay for an apartment for a few months. "Maybe it will be a fresh start for you. Maybe you'll be able to build something of yourself out there."

The loathing comes over him like a hot cloud, a long burning tongue licking up his spine. Does she not understand? Does she not know that his father left them, that he stopped loving them, that he's living with some Vietnamese bitch whose name they never even learned to pronounce, that his dad has new babies they haven't even met? The rage comes out cold: "You fucking bitch. You fucking bitch."

He retreats to the top floor and the internet. He types in "How far can you go in life when your mother is a bitch?" A Buzzfeed quiz pops up. His ordinary message boards are lit up with loathing for the President's listening tour. On the Boogaloo sites, he reads that the tour is a cover for preparations to impose martial law. The bitch President is on a reconnaissance mission. A listening tour is cover for why she's going to places that don't want her: to establish centers of control. It's part of the pedophile ring. The President is coming to town to organize the rape of children so she can black-mail the rapists. Everyone in power is in on it.

From the lower floor, the Assassin hears his mother whispering into the phone. "I don't know," she is saying. "I don't know what he's going to do." She's slowly weeping. "He's your son, too. You're responsible. You'll be responsible." Then: "No, no, no, you have to take him. You have to."

He goes to the vent in the attic and unscrews the panel. The black gun sits there like a small black bird waiting to fly. A secret. A gun is a time machine that changes the future.

The Final Stage of the Transition

The last step involves "intensification of pressure," according to Spaaij, a rising sense of urgency. Assassins tend to wither away in the weeks leading up to political murder. They stop talking to their families, stop responding to their emails. They give away precious objects and close out bank accounts. They detach themselves from people and objects. The reduce their lives to the roles they're about to perform.

"The Intensification of Pressure"

If the President doesn't die soon, all of America will descend into hell. There will be no hope for decent people. There will be no life for anyone like the Assassin. There will be no future. There is no future anyway. The Assassin rolls up the posters from his walls. He takes the Rubik's cube, the old typewriter. He wanders along his route to the library, drifts toward where the homeless have camped out. He remembers a little kid he's seen there before. The boy lives with his father and he's always fingering through a little box of treasures outside their tent. The Assassin has to search but he eventually finds him, staring into a phone, at the edge of the tent. He looks like he's just been crying. The Assassin leaves him the posters and other materials. "For you," he says to the surprised boy, and leaves.

He burns the rest of his stuff in a parking lot beside a failed shopping mall. That kid will know his name soon. He will be known. He and that homeless boy share the secret of his being.

Every morning, his mother wakes him up by knocking on his door and shouting, "We're going to have to talk tonight," but then she comes home and makes dinner. He comes down after she's eaten and eats. One morning he wakes up to find a plane ticket under the door, a one-way trip to San Jose. A Post-it note on top reads: "You don't have to go there but you can't stay here." There's another Post-it note underneath that Post-it: "It's for your own good." What his mother doesn't understand, what his father doesn't understand, is that he's a hero. They are the parents of a hero.

The Assassination Foiled

Every assassin has to be lucky. Gavrilo Princip, who shot the arch-duke Franz Ferdinand and ignited the First World War, only managed to reach his target because the archduke's Czech driver heard the driving instructions wrong, so instead of turning onto the Appel Quay, he proceeded onto Franz Joseph Street, where Princip was waiting. The course of history is full of flukes, especially when it comes to the business of killing particular individuals.

Just before the President arrives for her listening tour stop at the local high school where the Assassin graduated, the Assassin posts a political statement. It parrots various ideologies already inundating the internet, saving all the unborn babies, preserving American liberties, keeping America great. It celebrates guns above all. The title: "A Gun Is a Time Machine for the Future." Perhaps it will register on the Secret Service's machine learning algorithms. Perhaps not. It doesn't matter. The agents, guiding the President to the campaign stop, will be in complete control. Advance teams will have scouted every possible approach. Every angle of threat will have been established and neutralized. Every person in contact with the President will have been vetted. Security personnel will screen all points of access. Other security personnel will scan the crowd.

The Assassin wandering toward the President, gun snug in pocket, won't get close. There will be a crowd, both of locals and re-porters, and the President stops so briefly before entering the school that she's barely a glimpse before she's gone. That's it. That's the end. That's how much history the Assassin gets a look at. He will retreat and take comfort in a Jamba Juice across the street, a new despair settling over him. He wasn't meant to be a hero after all.

The Assassin will have to be lucky. But he doesn't have to be that lucky. All it would take would be for the President to decide, as she was driving away from the rally, to stop in at a Jamba Juice for a quick photo op. It's what the Secret Service calls an "off-the-record movement."

The Secret Service uses tradecraft to manipulate the environment in these situations as quickly as possible. They create barriers out of what's available. "We are always going to be in a position of advantage. We are never going to put the President into a position where we are at a disadvantage," my anonymous agent tells me. "What are the risks I'm willing to accept? Let's take the example of the President jumping out of a car and going into a diner. Well, I have to accept the risk. There are probably people who have some kind of weapon. Maybe it's a pocketknife. Maybe somebody has a handgun or two. For that initial move, I'm willing to accept it, and here's why. I also have the element of surprise on my side. No one knew he was coming." The people in the diner might have the means and the opportunity, but it's unlikely that they have nefarious intent. "It's such a low-probability event that I'm willing to accept that. Now, I'm only willing to accept that for a very short amount of time." It takes only a burst.

The Incident

Here is the moment that will be replayed endlessly. Multiple recordings will exist of this murder, from various surprised customers. The President extending her hand, laughing with an older couple, then the Assassin rising up with a blast from the little black Ruger, then the Secret Service tackling him.

The Possibility of Survival

The Assassin will need to have a good shot, with a bullet to the head or multiple to the body. "The Secret Service medical protocols are the most comprehensive in the world. Period," the agent tells me. "There's no other person who travels with a doctor twenty-four hours a day, with a physician assistant, combat-trained paramedic, and a nurse." Chemical, biological, and nuclear experts ride in every motorcade. "That's your baseline. That's the minimum." Beyond that extensive traveling team, agents plan out the medical contingencies of every journey, with a trauma center as close as possible. The President almost never ventures outside "the golden hour": advanced life support within the first hour of trauma. But not even the best team can save everyone every time.

The Immediate Aftermath

There, in the middle of some Jamba Juice, in the middle of the country, will be another assassinated President, another broken institution, another cracked symbol.

What would the aftermath of a presidential assassination look like today? "It would be incredibly pregnant with the potential for violence, because the society is so polarized," Ronald Eyerman, author of *The Cultural Sociology of Political Assassination,* and the world's foremost expert on national trauma in the aftermath of assassination, tells me. Typically, when democracies confront violent disruptions to the transition of power, they rely most heavily on their national symbols and collective rituals.

In other countries as well as in other eras of American history, moments of national unity and grief followed in the wake of assassinations. After Swedish prime minister Olof Palme was murdered on a main street of Stockholm in 1986, "there was a period when party politics was put aside and the nation mourned," Eyerman explains. The same thing happened after the assassination of both Kennedys, John and Robert. The current state of hyper-partisanship makes such solidarity almost inconceivable. "I don't think there would be a shock and a grieving. I think there would more likely be protest and collective violence," Eyerman says. "Then, in terms of the other representative figures, their performance in public would be extremely important." The representative figures of American politics, as we have seen, do not do bipartisanship. Rage primes popularity. Since hyper-partisanship has already afflicted every other political ritual, like the selection of Supreme Court justices, why wouldn't it overtake a presidential funeral?

"Especially with the history of violence in the US, and the prevalence of guns, and all the anger and frustration that's there, a spark like that is more likely to evoke violence than grieving," Eyerman notes. "One of the things that could happen is an institutional collapse, not only in terms of establishments but also in terms that would allow people to grieve." The next time a president is assassinated, the streets will not feature scenes of somber reflection. The streets will fill with rage and loathing, right on the edge of control.

What's One President More or Less?

As noted at the beginning of this dispatch, one in eleven American presidents has been assassinated. The country has survived all those assassinations. The next assassin doesn't matter. The president doesn't matter, either. This thought experiment serves to establish how different the meaning of a president is now. A president was once the unquestioned representative of the American people's will. The murder of that representative meant an assault on the nation as a whole.

Now there is no nation as a whole.

The Assassin as Hero

The Assassin would become a symbol, in direct inversion of the President. Just as the President would be a tyrant to half the country and an icon to the other half, the assassin would be a cold-blooded murderer to half the country and a heroic resister to the other half. The internet would throw up a fan club for him within hours. After Dylann Roof attacked the Emanuel African Methodist Episcopal Church, a "Bowl Gang" formed, in reference to his bowl haircut, on the hard-right social media sites Gab and Discord. And the established right-wing polarization network applies—from the internet, through mass media, to elected officials. After seventeen-year-old Kyle Rittenhouse killed Anthony Huber and Joseph Rosenbaum in Kenosha during a protest, the Republican Women of Waukesha County in Pewaukee gave his mother a standing ovation at a "safety and self-defense" event. Michelle Malkin, Republican pundit, talked to him on the phone, thanking him for his courage. Representative Thomas Massie of Kentucky praised Rittenhouse for his "incredible restraint and presence and situational awareness."

Presidential Mourning

The standard rituals of mourning will be followed. There will be a state funeral. The flags will fly at half-mast. But two new icons will have entered American public consciousness: the martyred President and the heroic Assassin. Meanwhile, a vice president will take over in turmoil and the sense of legitimacy in American democracy will plummet further. Who voted for him?

Hyper-Partisanship and the Decline of Institutional Legitimacy

An assassinated president would solidify the dominance of the executive role in American government. The end result would be an ever-hardening version of soft autocracy riddled with violent grievance politics born out of a sense of institutional illegitimacy. The Assassin and the President are both products of a hyper-partisan environment. In the current context, they would only be an external expression, an allegory of the violence that is overtaking the United States as symptomatic of the electoral process in mid-failure.

Democracies are built around institutions larger than partisan struggle; they survive on the strength of those institutions. "The delegitimization of national institutions inevitably leads to chaos," Scott Gates at PRIO says. Unfortunately, partisanship has already compromised nearly every institution in the United States. Congress has popularity numbers below 10 percent. The presidency, as it becomes less and less representative of the popular vote, loses its capacity to act with unified executive function. Since *Bush v. Gore* in 2000, everyone recognizes that the Supreme Court no longer represents transcendent interests of national purpose. It's merely a collection of partisan hacks, like any other branch of the US government.

Mitch McConnell's decision to make the appointment of a Supreme Court justice an election issue is a typical case of a political institution being converted into a token in a zero-sum game, exactly the kind of decision that destabilizes smaller, poorer countries struggling to maintain democracies. The norm of bipartisan agreement has been shattered forever and, once shattered, it cannot be put back together. Five of the nine current Supreme Court justices were appointed by presidents who lost the popular vote.

The cycle of negativity that has overtaken the American political process continually undermines trust in government. "Politics inherently evokes anger in America. It's a zero-sum game now," Steve Webster says. Anger and distrust make it virtually impossible to go about the business of governing, which leads to ineffective government, which reinforces the anger and distrust. Because of the widening distinction—the quite correct sense that *they* are not *us*—American politics has taken on more and more radical agendas, and because government is ineffective, why not? American politics behaves like an inverse pendulum, swinging farther to the extremes. Each side, divided by negative advertising, social media, and a primary system that encourages enthusiasm over reason, pursues ideological purity at any cost, because ideological purity increasingly leads to power. The actual business of governing is an afterthought.

No institutions stand above politics anymore—not the Supreme Court, not the FBI, not the Department of Justice, not the Centers for Disease Control (CDC), not the presidency. Faith in institutions of all types is on the decline: faith in religious leaders, police officers, business leaders, elected officials, journalists, university professors. When the crisis comes, the institutions won't be there.

The Next President

After taking the oath of office, the new president will give lengthy speeches, grand rhetoric about a time to heal, to build a unified country, to recover the glories of their history. He can say whatever he wants. It won't matter. He'll just be the necessary monster for half the country and the necessary idol for the other half.

Washington's Warning

Americans can't say they weren't warned. In his Farewell Address, George Washington was almost fantastically lucid about the exact situation the United States faces at this moment. "I have already intimated to you the danger of parties in the state, with particular reference to the founding of them on geographical discriminations . . . ," he warned. "This spirit, unfortunately, is inseparable from our nature, having its root in the strongest passions of the human mind. It exists under different shapes in all governments, more or less stifled, controlled, or repressed; but, in those of the popular form, it is seen in its greatest rankness and is truly their worst enemy." The greatest threat to the United States today is not the rise of the hard right. It is the general decline of legitimacy in government that underlies the rise of the hard right.

How did Washington see it? Why did he put so much emphasis of the rejection of partisanship? You have to remember that Washington gave his warning at the moment of supreme national and personal triumph. He wrote it, with Alexander Hamilton, at the end of his second term of office as he was preparing to return to Mount Vernon. His archenemy, King George III, had admitted in private that if Washington returned to his farm, "he will be the greatest man in the world." Washington had built an extraordinary country and was in the act of handing it over peacefully. Why, at this moment of personal moral supremacy, did he choose the dangers of partisanship as his subject?

Washington must have recognized the vulnerability that he himself had helped to create, the vulnerability inherent to the glory of the American experiment. Difference is the core of the American experience. Difference is its genius. There has never been a country—in history, in the world—so comfortable with difference, so full of difference. The great insight of its founders was that they based government not on the drive toward consensus but on the permission for disagreement. They structured American government to ensure as little domination by one faction as possible.

But the United States only works if there is a tension between the forces allowing difference and the forces insisting on unity. For 250 years, American legal and political institutions provided a system through which to negotiate its incomparable competition of interests and perspectives, and they created the greatest democracy and the greatest economy in the world. Once partisan drive takes precedence over the national interest, it shreds the tension underlying the system. Unless both sides believe that they're on the same side, they aren't. And once shared purpose disappears, it's gone. A flaw lurked right at the core of the experiment, as flaws so often do in works of ambitious genius.

The Farewell Address, every bit as powerful and important a document as any of the Founding Fathers' writings, was once as popular and as studied as the Declaration of Independence. Schoolchildren across America used to memorize and recite passages. But its popularity waned after the Second World War, when shared national purpose was an easy sell. Perhaps the time has come to revive the Farewell Address. Senators and congressmen and presidents would do well to listen to what Washington had to say: "The common and continual mischiefs of the spirit of party are sufficient to make it the interest and duty of a wise people to discourage and restrain it." At a Trump rally after the election, a reporter spotted a pair of Republicans wearing shirts that read, I'D RATHER BE A RUSSIAN THAN A DEMOCRAT. Centuries before, George Washington, riding out of thriving Philadelphia toward the lush hills of Mount Vernon, recognized what the failure of American democracy would look like. It looks like them.

The Grinding

Hate builds out of hate. Despair cascades. The rage out of which the Assassin will come is building, feeding on itself. The feeling of impotence and loss is by no means limited to one side or the other of the political spectrum. Nobody, or almost nobody, escapes the desperate trend. The parties have become consumed with defeating their opponents rather than building the country. Because of the domination of faction, government has separated from the business of policy. Meanwhile, the unifying myths and symbols that sustained the country for generations are crumbling. Explosions flare on the margins as the rot settles at the core. Hyperpartisanship shreds the party system, then it shuts down the legislative ability to enact policy, then it consumes the national symbols.

The Cost of Illegitimacy and Paralysis

Many Americans, as well as many outside America, once believed that America was different from any other country, that it was the culmination of history, the answer to history. They imagined that America represented something more than a country, an idea, a faith. We are finding out that America is only a part of history, that it rises and falls like everybody else. Its decaying political system will leave the United States more vulnerable than ever to shock and inaction just as it enters a period of unprecedented turbulence. Its government, at the best of times, was not designed to deal with the social, economic, and environmental crises it is about to face. The breakdowns in the political and information systems matter because they make it nearly impossible for the United States to deal with the coming emergencies. The fruit of hyper-partisanship and a toxic informational environment is paralysis—paralysis at a moment of peril.

The United States will soon enter a period of radical instability as a country, no matter who is in power and no matter what policies they enact. The economic future will be more volatile. The environmental future will be more unpredictable. The cities will be more vulnerable. The government will be incapable of policy and disconnected from the people's sense of their collective will.

As the country is torn apart by deep, intractable forces their leaders can do less and less to avoid or to mitigate, ordinary Americans will be torn apart with it.

THE FALL OF NEW YORK

There is politics. There is policy. Then there are people's lives. Assassination and rebellion are the dramas of the breakdown—but the causes of the drama and its ultimate effects are more subtle, more difficult to see. It's not just large American institutions that are vulnerable. American families are, too.

There is no such thing as a typical American family. America is much too diverse and, frankly, much too weird to produce anything so fixed. For this dispatch, I have imagined two related families, one multicultural, coastal, and urban; the other white, central, and rural. These two sisters, one in New York and the other in Iowa, while by no means an adequate proxy for the country, represent the dangers across the main political and economic and geographic division in the country.*

The catastrophes are coming for everyone. They will seem to come out of a blue sky.

The Coming of the Storm

In the late summer, the NOAA (National Oceanic and Atmospheric Administration) National Hurricane Center upgrades its hurricane watch to a hurricane warning. The storm forming in

---

* While there's no such thing as a typical American family, there is an average one, and I've tried to reflect the average in family structure and jobs. The average American family has 3.14 members. Half of American marriages end in divorce.

the mid-Atlantic, picking up power from hot, moist conditions, needs a name: Muriel. New York goes about its business as usual. The name that will come to mean the end of the city is just another name.

Nobody cancels their trips to the Hamptons because of Muriel. The psychiatrists still take their month off. The Yankees have to cancel their series with the Blue Jays, but in the sweltering of New York in August, the idea of a solid rain seems, to some, like it might offer a break, refreshment. They have the wall by then. That's the source of New York's confidence. The Greater Manhattan Seawall, conceived after Superstorm Sandy and costing up-

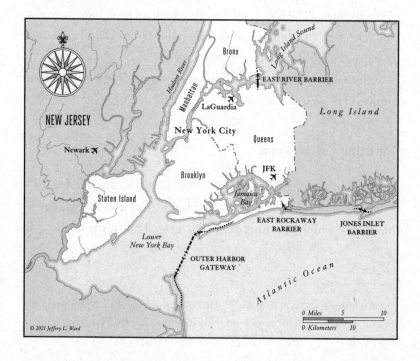

wards of $119 billion,* will have already prevented several storm surges up to Category 3. As the storm comes on, they will close the gates at the East Rockaway Barrier, the Jones Inlet Barrier, and the East River Barrier.

The Seawall embraces the city like the arms of a protective father. It makes the city feel safe.

The following afternoon, under dark skies, the Governor gives a press conference: "For most families in the Tri-state area, the correct decision is to evacuate. If you have family away from the coasts, if you can find a place to stay in the interior, go there," he says. "If you make the decision to stay, please prepare. Gas and electricity will be subject to massive interruptions. Most of the conveniences that you take for granted will not be available. If you know of any handicapped people, any elderly people, who have not found access to services, help them find those resources." Most New Yorkers take the Governor's statement as tacit encouragement not to evacuate. It's the standard statement before a storm, and superstorms on the Eastern Seaboard are no longer a rarity.

One of the New Yorkers listening to the Governor's warning is a producer at WNYC, the local public radio station. She works mainly on the daily pop culture and politics podcast, but

---

* In February 2020, the Trump administration called a halt to the building of the New York Harbor Storm-Surge Barrier. At the moment of writing, the Army Corps of Engineers considers the project "indefinitely postponed." Another way of putting that statement is that New York's safety has been indefinitely postponed. I have conceived of this Dispatch under the assumption that the basic sanity of the Seawall proposal will eventually prevail. This is a significant assumption. Needless to say, if the Seawall is not built, New York will be vastly more exposed than the description in this Dispatch.

she makes occasional documentaries, too. Like every other New York, she worries about Muriel but not enough to change her plans. The Producer lives in Gowanus in a two-bedroom with her husband and their teenage daughter. The place is smaller than they would like, but they never had an opportunity to find better. They were too busy living through Covid, and then the crash, and then the drought. When the storm first sets in, she has an idea for a story, an audio essay, a kind of *This American Life*-style piece, about riding out a storm in New York, a combination of personal confession with an up-close investigation of the effects of climate change. They send journalists to war zones. How bad could New York get?

The Producer and her husband talk it over. At first they can't see a reason for any of them to leave. But the city's sticky with the heat and she wants to be alone to produce the piece, and the sound of her husband and child in the background would be complicating. Besides, her daughter hasn't seen her grandmother since the Thanksgiving before. So the husband and daughter head out to Iowa for a couple of weeks while the Producer stays in New York. They have to take the train down to Philadelphia for the flight because the airports in New York are too full. The Producer's sister, unemployed and living with their mother, doesn't understand why they all don't just move to Iowa. The Heartland is safe for them, at least from hurricanes.

The Precariousness of the Twenty-First Century

Right now, at this moment, wherever you happen to be, you live in a period of cheap food and safe cities in an orderly world. The cheapness and the safety and the order cannot last. The systems by which we go about our lives, and which we take for granted, are growing more threadbare. America's paralyzed and half-legitimate government won't be able to respond with adequate measures. The radical instability will have political consequences. Climate crises and mass inequality have been preludes to civil war and to revolution everywhere—Europe, Africa, South America, Asia—and they'll be preludes to crisis in the United States as well. But the consequences of the new instability transcend politics. Over the next fifty years, American lives are destined to become much more precarious. Some lives will shatter.

The Three Principal Threat Multipliers

Economic and environmental instability are what the US military calls "threat multipliers," destabilizing forces that brew underneath the surface. The instability feeds into the chaos and rage that explodes. There are three principal threat multipliers facing the United States today: economic inequality, drought, and property vulnerability.

The Boredom Problem

One of the reasons why the stability crises of the twenty-first century are stubbornly difficult to solve is because they're boring. They don't make good stories. The forces that threaten to destroy the world don't have faces. They offer no satisfying conflict between protagonist and antagonist. Inequality and climate change are collective failures requiring collective solutions. Who survives and what survives and in what condition they survive will be determined by the dreariest of questions: taxation levels and environmental regulation on an international level. Their dreariness has consequences; ordinary people don't care.

The Democracy Problem

Inequality and climate change will cause the disasters that ordinary Americans are going to feel most acutely. They already do. But to address these problems requires massive, concerted political action, both domestically and internationally. And the United States can't even convince its citizens not to drink at bars during a plague. Democracy—as a system balancing the rights of individuals with the interests of the state—contains inherent limits on collective action: the American political system, with its structure of checks and balances, was never designed to deal with collective crises. In its current state of hyper-partisanship, the US government is effectively paralyzed. One of democracy's deepest flaws is that no one gets elected for catastrophes they're going to prevent. Even after foreseeable catastrophes strike, Americans tend to forgive their leaders. They, too, didn't want to believe the worst was coming.

Covid as a Pretest

Covid represents exactly the problems facing the twenty-first century. It's not an enemy with a face but a crisis of systems. Controlling Covid required scientific consensus, effective policy, and social solidarity. Countries that came to the wrong scientific consensus, like Sweden, suffered. Countries that enacted the wrong policies, like England, suffered. Countries with low levels of solidarity, like Russia, suffered. The American response to Covid was unique. Of all countries with populations higher than 5 million and at least $25,000 per capita gross domestic product, the United States had the highest death rate. Political dysfunction was the obvious cause.

If you were to ask, "What was America's Covid response?" you would get no answer. Part of the government said to wear masks, while part of it banned them. Even the most basic questions of public health became toxic: mask deniers and mask proponents physically attacked one another. At a moment when the safety of each individual required the most basic collective action—"Wear a mask"—Americans refused to stop infighting, even though their infighting led to higher risks for everybody and mass death. Failure to listen to scientists and failure to act on their insights have consequences. And, in the case of Covid, the science was clear, the cost of action was low, and the consequences were direct. Compared to the crises that are coming, Covid was nothing. Covid has been like an easy pop quiz before a punishing final exam.

The Covid Thanksgiving

As she waits for the storm to hit New York, the Producer remembers the Covid Thanksgiving—the Thanksgiving right after Biden was elected. Nationally, Covid had reached the beginning of its third wave, with a little more than 200,000 cases and 2,000 deaths a day. Pfizer had announced a vaccine, but it had yet to be approved. Unemployment had steadied at 14.7 percent. One in nine Americans were on food stamps. The CDC urged people to stay home, not to travel, but nobody seemed to be paying attention. Even though she trusted the CDC, even though she knew better, they went home for Thanksgiving that year. The Producer felt they had to. Her mother hadn't seen the baby.

She wasn't a producer at WNYC then, just an audio freelancer. Her husband was making good money as a web designer. They had their little girl in February, a few weeks before Covid overran the hospitals. So many of her friends fled to the country, or to other countries, but they had to stay. They needed their in-network clinic. She remembered they ran out of places to bury the dead on Hart Island. Then the businesses started closing: Dizzy's Diner went down, and her favorite, Cocoa Bar in Park Slope, too. Still, she felt safer in the city. A friend in Wyoming wore a mask in a grocery store, and a guy in the parking lot screamed at her, "Why do you believe all that Communist horseshit?"; she ended up driving to Colorado for groceries. The Producer's sister back home didn't believe Covid was real.

Home, for the Producer, would always be the farmhouse her great-grandfather built at the turn of the twentieth century in the cornfields outside Davenport, Iowa. The family called it the Big House. If she closes her eyes, she can still see herself running down from her childhood bedroom on the third floor, past the window on the stairs where the rich wood of the dark paneling gave out to the limitless fields of swaying corn, through the front door, and to the bus for school. Her great-grandfather had overseen every detail of the Big House's construction, designed it to the specifications of the large Eastern properties he had envied as a poor boy growing up in Vermont. A real estate agent might describe the place as a large five-bedroom in the Federal style with a classic wraparound porch—if the property weren't so remote that no real estate agent would ever have a reason to describe it. When her father had decided to switch from farming to insurance, he sold most of the surrounding acreage to the neighbors, which they, in turn, sold onto corporate agribusinesses, but the Producer's parents kept living in the Big House. When her father died suddenly in his sixties from a brain aneurysm brought on by lymphoma, her mom stayed on, though the Big House needs more upkeep than a single elderly woman could properly provide. The Big House is the family's piece of America.

When the Producer made the decision to return to Iowa during Covid, her sister set them up with a trailer behind the Big House. That year her sister's boyfriend had left for the Dakotas, looking for work, and she started the job at the Ram dealership, and his trailer was available. The Producer agreed with her husband that it would be best to have limited contact with the Iowa side of the family, to keep six feet apart, not to enter the Big House. But within a few minutes, those rules, so carefully negotiated, were all broken. Her mom had to cuddle the new baby. Her niece and nephew, who were six and four then, wanted their hugs too.

Mom prepared the classic American feast. They had a sixteen-pound turkey and pork chops and sausages. The family macaroni and cheese, made with nutmeg. Tater crumble, cheese on ground beef on tater tots. And the harvest of the backyard garden: mashed potatoes with gravy, and beans and peas and beets and corn and carrots and shredded cabbage cooked with pork. For dessert, they had Swedish pastries, cinnamon cookies, and a tusenbladstårta, a thousand-layered torte—traditions inherited from some forgotten Scandinavian ancestor. As they sat down to eat, they viewed the future with hope even in the middle of plague. Maybe life would return to normal? They weren't doing too bad for Covid. Car sales had risen 6.2 percent over the year, so the dealership was flourishing. Her sister had to greet customers behind plexiglass, which she didn't mind. With a mask on, she could say what she liked and nobody was sure what she'd said.

The sisters didn't know, because nobody ever knows, that these were the good times.

The First Threat Multiplier: Inequality

You know the problem of inequality is serious when rich people have started to worry that they're too rich. In the United States, the wealthiest of the ultrawealthy, the kind who wouldn't notice $10 million one way or another, are forming political action committees opposed to the concentration of wealth in their own hands. The Patriotic Millionaires formed in 2010 with two extraordinary goals: to lobby politicians to increase their taxes, and to explain to ordinary Americans how unjust the economic order is. Two of the richest men in the world, Bill Gates and Warren Buffett, have publicly called on the government to raise their tax rates. "I have a message for my fellow filthy rich, for all of us who live in our gated bubble worlds," warned early Amazon investor Nick Hanauer in 2014. "Wake up, people. It won't last." He couldn't be more right. The Koch brothers have recently shifted their charitable endeavors from libertarian politics to the problem that the new generation will be worse off than the old.

The rich know what historians know: every society in human history with levels of inequality like those in the United States today has descended into war, revolution, or plague. No exceptions. There are precisely zero historical precedents that don't end in destruction. Since 1980, inequality has been growing globally, but in the United States the growth is most dramatic. In 2015, the top 1 percent of American families made 26.3 times what the 99 percent did, garnering 22 percent of all income—the highest share since the peak of 23.9 percent before the Great Depression. In 1965, a CEO made roughly twenty times the typical worker's pay. Now it's 271 times. From 1980 on, the poorest 50 percent of the population has consistently seen a decline in their share of income. American inequality is now worse than it was in 1774.

All of the political loathing in the first two dispatches of this book, the hyper-partisanship and disunion, the sheer rage—all of it dates, in large part, from the 2008 financial crisis. That's when sovereign citizenry spiked; that's when negative partisanship, the Tea Party and Occupy Wall Street, originated.

The Effect of Income Inequality on Market Cycles

Economic models are, at best, weakly predictive. Covid, again, provided a good test. Not one analyst of note predicted that the economy would crater, unemployment would spike, and then the stock market would rise. That prediction wouldn't have made any sense. A crash is coming, though. It always is: Look at 2008, 2001, 1987, 1973, 1966, 1929, 1907, 1901, 1857, 1837, 1819, 1792, 1763, and 1640. Crashes are an inevitable feature of modern capitalist economies. Capitalism works in cycles or, to be precise, it has always so far worked in cycles. Extreme inequality makes a market crash much more likely and a recovery much more difficult.

What will life look like just before the crash? It will look like right now. At the time of writing, the long-term yields on government bonds have fallen below the short-term yields on government bonds. This condition, which should be an economic impossibility, has predicted a major crash in every previous occurrence in history. Some sovereign bonds have a negative yield, which means the lender pays the borrower for the loan. If this sounds like it doesn't make sense, that's because it doesn't. Most asset classes worldwide—equities, bonds, real estate, commodities—are approaching all-time-high prices. With interest rates at a hard low, no market correction in recent memory, and the expectation that the Fed will always inject more money no matter what the crisis, people and companies are borrowing too much. Once borrowers can no longer repay loans, loan values collapse. If the values of their assets drop, their own lenders start calling in loans or refuse to lend them new money. That's how death spirals start.

The standard policies for alleviating financial crises—lowering interest rates, cutting taxes, and quantitative easing—will all be unavailable because of current US policy. Interest rates cannot be lowered any further. In Europe, they have recently begun the practice of negative interest rates. In the United States, the cost of borrowing money is slightly above zero. Similarly, American taxes are at historic lows and deficits are at record highs. Quantitative easing, once an emergency measure, is now standard practice. The amount of cash in the financial system today is about four times as much as in mid-2008. Nobody knows why or how the crash will come, but when it does come, there will be highly limited room to move. The Federal Reserve will be "out of bullets."

Jonathan D. Ostry, deputy director of the research department at the International Monetary Fund, knows the dangers of inequality to any economy. Low inequality is emerging as a part of the Washington consensus, the conservative credo of macroeconomics. Even they have figured out that inequality strangles economies. The right-wing consensus has been that free trade, moderate marginal tax rates, and low interest rates lead to longer periods of growth. They do. But Ostry's research, undertaken before the Arab Spring, before the Occupy movement, found that, as Ostry says, "low levels of inequality are robustly protective of growth duration. High levels of inequality seem to be associated, in all different times and all different countries, with the premature end of a growth spell. This is a striking finding." From a policy point of view, neither increasing inequality nor decreasing inequality are good in themselves. Both can lead to deeper prosperity and stability: when China decreased its redistribution of wealth, the move sparked growth; when Brazil increased its level of redistribution that, too, sparked growth. For most of the world, about three-quarters of the countries Ostry studied, increasing redistribution would increase growth and preserve the length of growth. The United States belongs to that group.

Inequality makes it vastly more difficult to deal with the fallout of a crash. "Think of a society that's very unequal and bumping along, experiencing decent economic growth, and suddenly something bad happens to it, an oil shock or a virus or its biggest banks go under or it has a typhoon or whatever, and growth collapses," Ostry says. "That could be a blip and it could get back on its feet very rapidly. The way you would avoid having this bad shock turn into something more sinister [is] you would have to adjust economic policies, and whenever you make such adjustments, there can be pain. The buy-in from the population for the kind of adjustments needed to get the economy back on its feet—there is much less buy-in in unequal societies." If society's wealth has accrued to the top 1 percent during periods of growth, then the other 99 percent don't have any incentive to sign on for short-term pain if they're still going to live in a society where the top 1 percent prosper exclusively. Inequality lessens social cohesion. "That sounds airy-fairy but it's really supported in the data," Ostry says. "When you're very unequal, there's not just inequality of outcomes but inequality of opportunities. People are not going to have access to health care, to education, to the political process, so you're going to be leaving a lot of your population disenfranchised and not participating. It's going to mean that your economy is being run by a very small group. Those societies are going to be more brittle and less resilient to shocks." Inequality leads to crashes, which lead to further inequality.

Bailouts are inevitably unfair. People who have saved suffer most. The irresponsible are the first to receive relief. As governments decrease spending, cutting into Social Security and Medicare, it is the poorest who lose the most. Typically, in unequal societies, financial markets are eager to extend credit to people who can't afford to service their loans. The borrowers have a low capacity to consume and must borrow to sustain their consumption. The buildup of debt fuels vulnerabilities in financial markets. Inequality feeds into crisis, which feeds into inequality.

Inequality as a Problem Without a Solution

Inequality has no solution. Even extreme efforts at redistribution, for which there is little to no political appetite in the United States currently, tend only to slow inequality's rise. Even communism only decreased inequality by destroying wealth. But you don't need prediction to know that the American economic system is entering a deeply contradictory state. Economic growth has been artificially raised to a fever pitch, while life expectancy has been in decline for three years—a first for an advanced economy in history. Each subsequent American generation does worse than its predecessor. The current American generation will feel the decline over the course of their lives.

The Depression Thanksgiving

She had just started as a producer at WNYC the year of the crash. She couldn't afford to go home, but she did anyway. That was the Thanksgiving after the Big One, after the run on the banks and the deflation of prices. The suicide rate was at 39.3 per 100,000 people. Nearly one-third of American families qualified as "food insecure." She never forgot going to the bank, putting in her card, and seeing it spat out. She called the bank and a cheerful artificial voice told her that the next available agent would take her call in thirty-seven hours. She remembered the scenes of chaos: the police managing the lines outside one of the failed banks with their guns drawn, the hand grenades thrown into Goldman Sachs. In Jimmy's Corner, a boxer bar near Times Square, she listened to a pack of coked-up finance bros discuss the most effective and popular ways to commit suicide. (She remembers thinking suicide was a good option for them.) Overnight, the tech companies decamped to Amsterdam and the financial services industry to Connecticut compounds. The Producer's husband found a better rate out of the Buffalo airport, so they drove up from the city at 3:30 in the morning. They landed in Iowa in the afternoon, exhausted.

The panic of the unfolding crisis had not so much cooled as normalized by Thanksgiving. Each crisis of confidence in the markets, staggering in just after the last, eroded a little further the security of the system as a whole. Her husband's graphic design work had dried to a trickle, and looking for a job was harder than any job: the exhaustion of drifting into despair, then lugging himself out of it.

The cousins ran in a pack around the property. To her daughter, who had only ever known the cramped spaces of tiny Brook-

lyn apartments, the Big House was still a magical place. The idea
that there could be houses with so many rooms that some of them
were empty seemed like something from a show. The fields outside, ragged and bare as they were in November, lightly dusted
with snow, seemed as good as infinity. The Producer's nephew
was unusually quiet, mostly sitting on his own and staring at the
television in a kind of daze. Earlier that year he had been sent
home from school with pink eye, or what everybody thought was
pink eye. His mom kept putting in the drops like the pharmacist
told her to. There wasn't a lot of yellow gunk around the eye,
so she thought the drops were working. She couldn't take him
to the local doctor anyway. She couldn't afford the deductible. A
few days later, because she didn't want to take a day off work,
she brought the boy to the emergency room. They took one look,
rushed him past the waiting room, and attached him to intrave-
nous antibiotics. It wasn't pink eye. It was periorbital cellulitis.
The poor boy went blind in his left eye. The bill came to $43,000.
He might have had neurological damage, too, but her sister didn't
have the money to run the test.

The sisters didn't talk about money. The subject was too tense.
The Producer was hanging on in New York. The Ram dealership
hadn't fired her sister but they cut everybody's wages.

That year, for something different, their mother roasted a couple of chickens from the yard, but they still had the tater crumble
and the nutmeg mac and cheese, the mashed potatoes, with gravy,
the bread stuffing, and beans and peas and beets and corn and carrots and shredded cabbage cooked with pork. Then after that there
was the tusenbladstårta and also Jell-O because it was the boy's
favorite.

They had a lot to be grateful for. As they gathered around the table in the long dining room, the children were growing. Nobody was out on the streets. They had enough to eat. They were the lucky ones.

The Precision of Climate Change Modeling

This book draws on all the best available models of the future—economic forecasts, agronomic projections, established battle plans, algorithms from political scientists, historical patterns from scholars of civil war, and so on. But the climate change models that follow are vastly more concrete and precise than anything else in this book. They don't predict the future; they portray it. The first climate model appeared in 1967, created by Syukuro Manabe and Richard T. Wetherald, and it remains more or less completely accurate. They predicted that a doubling of CO_2 in the atmosphere would raise the temperature of the atmosphere by about 2°C. We have collectively increased CO_2 in the atmosphere by 50 percent since the 1880s and the temperature has risen by nearly 1°C.

The Limits of Climate Change Models

Knowing the general trend is not the same as knowing the outcome. Manabe himself described the limited power of his model: "Models have been very effective in predicting climate change, but have not been as effective in predicting its impact on ecosystems and human society." That climate change exists and will produce higher temperatures and rising sea levels is not debatable. The consequences of warming temperatures and rising sea levels on people remain largely unknown because our reactions are not yet set: How will nations and states mitigate climate change? How will communities adapt? What are the limitations of adaptation?

Bernhard Schauberger, a researcher at the Potsdam Institute for Climate Impact Research, understands the oversimplification of most models of climate change. For one thing, "there is no such thing as a global temperature," he points out. For convenience, everybody says that the global mean temperature rise will be between 4° and 6°C, but the rise is greater closer to the poles, and the rise in the temperate zones will be more rapid than in tropical zones. Higher temperatures lead to more heat waves, more droughts. But can you blame climate change when a fire consumes a small town in California? No one can say directly. It's like smoking. No doctor can say that if you smoke you will certainly get cancer, that the cigarettes gave you cancer. But the doctors do know that if you smoke, the chances of cancer are much higher.

Extremity is on its way. Or, rather, "what is now extreme will be normal in fifty years," Schauberger says. The Indian monsoon was very predictable forty or fifty years ago. It is no longer. The same movement into chaos is happening in the United States. The atmosphere becomes less predictable, producing long periods without precipitation, followed by torrential rains. The July 2012 drought is the most recent example of what extreme weather can do to agricultural systems. The losses due to drought that year were estimated at $30 billion. The direct cost was a 6 percent increase in the price of international food commodities. The price of corn rose 50 percent and that of soybeans 35 percent. That was a once-in-a-generation drought, although "once-in-a-generation" does not mean what it once meant. Already, the dramatic warming trend over the past four decades has led to devastating flash droughts in the high plains and the prairies.

The Second Threat Multiplier: Drought

Jerry Hatfield is the laboratory director of the National Laboratory for Agriculture and the Environment in Ames, Iowa, and he has been with the USDA for thirty-five years. He has lived through the great realization about climate change: "When I graduated with my PhD in 1975 from the University of California, Davis, I was trying to figure out the impact of cooling temperatures on agriculture." Back in the seventies, they were worried about the return of glaciers. "If you stay around long enough, you can work both sides of the issues," he says.

At first, even as the rise in temperature began to register, it was unclear whether increases in heat would damage agriculture. In the 2000s, temperature increases offset the effect of CO_2. (CO_2 is good for plants, "weeds in particular.") Since then, each subsequent report from the Intergovernmental Panel on Climate Change, a United Nations body, has grown more and more grim. The most recent report from the IPCC is a plea for keeping the level of warming below 2°C and a warning that the worst impacts may be inevitable after 2030.

The rising heat poses a problem particularly for commodity crops like corn, rice, and soybeans. Organic enzymes don't function beyond 40°C. The primary effect of heat is to deprive plants of water, lowering biomass and yields. Heat results in senescence of leaves—aging before they have reached their potential. High temperature levels affect germination and pollination. In 2012, during the drought year, western Kansas and Nebraska were so hot that even irrigated fields could not maintain enough water to keep the plants out of water stress. "They just could not physically pump enough water through the plant," Hatfield says. "What we think is that if we continued on these trends of increased temperature, variability, and precipitation, past 2050 we're going to have much more adaptation."

Heat harms wheat, too. "On wheat, what we find is that there won't be any grain on the ear," Hatfield observes. High heat doesn't hurt perennial crops like fruit. But the lack of lower temperatures does. Perennial crops in the Central Valley of California require a certain number of chilling hours. They have to be exposed to temperatures below 7°C before they will flower the next spring. These trees can no longer meet the number of hours required to get an effective "fruit set." Hatfield notes that "if it takes thirty years to breed a perennial tree—say, a pear or a cherry—this could be quite catastrophic in terms of fruit production. The question is: Do you move perennial orchards? Or do you think about adaptation strategies? Can we chemically treat that tree to think it's been chilled? What do we do with this process to understand the dynamics of what's going on?"

Vegetables will survive: "They can be moved around. There are strategies that are there," Hatfield says, but overall, climate change will wreak havoc across the world's farms. When waters rise and fields flood, roots have difficulty getting oxygen. Fungi and pathogens like heat. Diseases that tend to die off in cold winters will persist year-round. Livestock suffer in heat. The milk production of cows decreases.

The Adaptive Capacity of the American Farmer

Farmers will adapt to climate. That's what farmers do. And do not underestimate the adaptive capacity of the American farmer. In the first third of the twentieth century, the average corn yield was

1.6 metric tons per hectare. Now it is approaching 9.5 metric tons per hectare. For many commodity crops, adaptation is already underway. The rice agronomists and producers started to notice that they were getting lower yields with higher temperatures, so they selected for rice varieties that pollinate during the early morning. They can do the same for wheat and barley. But corn doesn't work that way. In corn, the pollen has to migrate from the tassel to the silks, a three foot distance. "The real impact is on the pollination phase," Hatfield says. "You got these little pollen grains out there in the air as they travel from the male to the female part of the plant. If they're exposed to high temperatures, that tends to destroy their viability." In corn, temperatures above 30°C have a negative impact. So if they're pollinating in the afternoon at 35°C, they will fail. Hatfield points out that, "sometimes, the high temperatures are coupled with extremely dry environments, so that pollen grain gets desiccated as well. That's where you end up with bare spots on the corncob." Corn is to food what plastic is to the material world: it's used in sweeteners, food fillers, emulsifiers, preservatives, adhesives. Since the invention of high-fructose corn syrup in 1958, corn has dominated the American food system as a whole. Any substantial impact on corn production will affect the entire food supply chain.

Rising temperatures also cause droughts, or, in the agronomist's phrase, the heat "increases atmospheric demand." Water leaves the plant with a higher transpiration rate. In 2012, farmers had to access the water in the Ogallala Aquifer, which is not a sustainable resource. "There is a concern about how long the water will last," Hatfield says. "The Ogallala Aquifer, which underlies the great plains from South Dakota all the way to Texas, has been shrinking over the past decades. That has forced producers to go to drip irrigation rather than full-scale sprinkler irrigation, but that water's not replenished. That's primordial water. It's not even well understood how it ended up there in the first place." Huge amounts of water currently used in American agriculture are nonrenewable: "Once it's gone, it's gone," Hatfield says. It's not possible to adapt to no water.

The Innovation Trap

American farmers, in their brilliance, will probably be able to adapt to rising temperatures, and even to increases in variability of water. What scares Hatfield is the chart of May–June precipitation compared against July–August precipitation. "Those patterns are unlike anything we've seen in 125 years," he says. "We're kind of in uncharted territory."

The great innovative splurge in agriculture since the end of the Second World War, the Green Revolution, resulted from increased genetic material, increased inputs from nitrogen, and refined pesticides. A stable climate made all of those innovations possible. With a stable climate, innovative farmers could breed for higher nitrogen uptake. "There seems to be a tradeoff between high yield and high stability," says Hatfield, who is pessimistic. High-yield crops have higher sensitivity to drought and heat.

How can you adapt to inconsistency? How can you adapt to what you can't imagine? Adaptation requires time and consistency. Designing new crop cycles takes thirty years or more. You can do them in ten or fifteen, Hatfield says, if you rush. "When Monsanto releases a new variety, it has been tested for quite a long time, and this is a fundamental problem with adaptation. The speed of climate change may be faster than breeding can cope with." The crisis in American farming will be an innovation trap. "One of the key components of adaptation is that you need to know what to adapt to. So, is it to one degree of climate change? Is it two? Three? Four?" The best adaptation, and also the easiest, would be to stop climate change. The easiest adaptation is the least likely.

Stable yields have already started to move north. Heat-tolerant cultivars, drought-tolerant cultivars, and expanded irrigation are all in the works. But the larger part of agricultural land in the United States is rain-fed. "What are the degrees of freedom that we're going to have? Is the environment going to be such that we won't be able to cope?" Hatfield asks. The real danger is unpredictability itself. "Mother nature is a very fickle lady," he says. "Producers ask me all the time, 'What's normal anymore?' I tell them basically we're out on the fringes. Producers say 'Yeah, I already know that. What do I do? What do I do about this beast that's staring me in the face whenever I plant a crop?'" Their current anxiety is all under the assumption that the predictive models stay within historical limits. The farther into the future you look, the higher the inconsistency, the greater the variability, the more intense the vulnerability.

The Effect of Decreased American Yields

The consequences of agricultural instability will reach far beyond America's borders. American abundance spills out all over the rest of the world. The United States is, by far, the world's largest exporter of food. The catastrophe of a drought on the world's 800 million subsistence farmers would be extreme, a famine. The great gift of America's agricultural ingenuity is reaching its apogee.

"The rate at which we're changing, that may be quicker than what we anticipated," Hadfield suggests. "It's tough to see where we go fifty or a hundred years from now."

The Politics of Hunger

Multiple droughts in a row are not unknown to the Midwest. The 1930s had four. Those droughts were not the result of incompetent farming; rather, the opposite. The Dust Bowl was a direct result of the newly invented deep-plowing methods that allowed the Great Plains to produce the vast quantities of cheap food that enabled, among other triumphs, the American victory in the First World War. The innovative prosperity of deep-plowing methods had a catastrophic reckoning built into it. The topsoil blew away. There were food riots. Americans died of starvation. Food shortages produced elevated levels of murder, suicide, and robbery.

Americans have not forgotten the hunger of that period. It informs some of America's deepest food trends. Country gravy, for example—powdered milk, flour, oleo—dates from the Depression, a cheap way to provide calories from the most basic available ingredients. "Aunt Sammy," the government-mandated promoter from the USDA's Bureau of Home Economics, introduced the notion of whole wheat during the Dust Bowl, a healthier option but also a cheaper one. She taught ways of fancying up split-pea soup with a slice of lemon. Before the Depression, American families traditionally served a bevy of pies with Thanksgiving dinner: mincemeat, cranberry, huckleberry. There would be a chicken pie along with the turkey and vegetables of all kinds. Aunt Sammy, in her Thanksgiving menu, suggested tomato juice instead of oyster stew, and no turkey but a roast or an "old hen" or "mock duck"—flank steak spread with bread crumbs rolled up, seared, then baked.

The United States already eats a post-Depression diet. The Depression brought vitamins and calories to the American consciousness. There was a rush on canning and pickling. "Go back to the 1930s; the Dust Bowl was four or five drought years in a row. Look at West Texas, western Kansas, right now: they've had four years of low precipitation in a row," Hatfield points out. "These things that are way below normal are happening. They're not widespread, but they are occurring."

Even slight spikes in the price of other commodities, like crude oil, has led to unrest the world over. The Yellow Vest movement in France, the country's most pronounced political violence since 1968, exploded from a relatively small rise in the price of gasoline. For highly unequal societies, any commodity price increase creates a threat to stability.

For ordinary Americans, instability will mean hunger.

The Drought Thanksgiving

The Producer never knew hunger, not even after the third drought in five years. Nearly two-thirds of American families qualified as "food insecure" by then. The number of Americans using their savings to buy food was 28 million and growing. The first year, the drought had barely made the news, small items in the financial papers about the rise in food prices. Even her sister hadn't worried much the first year. The second year of drought was when the anxieties drifted down, from the experts and the farmers, to ordinary people. The drought two years later was when the prices spiked.

One day, the Producer picked up a Napa cabbage that cost $28.

It's a beautiful cabbage but not that beautiful, she thought. Around that time, she realized that they were keeping almond milk behind the counter. Soldiers in full military gear moonlighted for Walmart. New York suddenly flourished with gardens, the Drought Gardens. In Brooklyn, every rooftop, every veranda—every bit of backyard—had tomatoes and lettuce and herbs. How best to grow your vegetables became one of those permanent topics of conversation, like real estate and school districts, and when her colleagues at WNYC or the parents of her daughter's school friends found out she was from Iowa, they assumed she was more or less a farmer, asking for advice as if she knew. She did find herself dreaming of the garden in Iowa in the days leading up to the Drought Thanksgiving.

She had to take the bus back to Davenport. She justified it as a bonding opportunity with her teenage daughter, just the two of them riding cross-country. It was the only way they could afford to go. Her husband couldn't stomach a thirty-two-hour bus ride. He stayed in New York that year.

The road trip was supposed to be educational, but not as educational as it turned out to be. Every town on the thirty-two-hour trip to Davenport was dying. The bus stations in the smaller places seemed to be placed there out of habit. The diners, which doubled as cleaning stations and brothels, weren't safe even in daylight. In the fields, the corn was stunted, brownish yellow in the rows, the spaces too wide. Where once there was planned lushness, now there was simply empty space. Herds of feral hogs ravaged the landscape. A mound of clothes had been dumped beside a boarded-up school. They passed through a town where recently thirty-two people had died from drinking vodka that had been cut with ethyl alcohol. The Producer didn't let her daughter

THE FALL OF NEW YORK

leave the bus, even when she whined about her cramped legs. Mostly they just sat in the back watching movies on a phone with a split audio cable. The prairies were so ragged there wasn't much to see.

The Big House was full up then. Her sister and the kids had moved in after the Ram dealership closed. The only work her sister could find was temporary room cleaning on a contract basis with the local Red Roof. It offered no benefits or security. Her niece had the grades to go to college but she would have had to borrow nearly half a million dollars to attend. In the meantime, she found herself working beside her mother on the carts. Any little bit of money helped. As for the boy, he was still in school, but after the austerity program had been put in place, classroom sizes swelled to sixty kids. There was no help for kids with learning difficulties. He was almost a young man then. He had developed an obsession with the military, making models of panzers and Hamilton bombers in his room. Bright red Nazi and Allied propaganda screamed from the walls. The army would never take him because of his eye. He brought the fact up in nearly every conversation. They had all started to fear her nephew, with his menacing silences and the angry hopelessness flaring up in bursts.

Her mother's garden had expanded. Even in drought, she could eke out beets and carrots and a row of lettuce. The Producer wondered if she could make a show out of her mother's garden: the simple prosperity of abundant greens. It was what everyone was talking about in New York, anyway. *The Garden*. Might work.

Thanksgiving dinner had changed with the drought. They used to eat turkey, but turkeys are corn-fed and so, much too expensive. The tater crumble, the nutmeg mac and cheese, the tusenbladstårta with its cream filling—they're mostly corn and therefore quite expensive. They skipped the mac and cheese and tater crumble but they had to have the tusenbladstårta. The year of the drought, her mother experimented with soy turkey, which was tasty enough, though it had a slight chemical tinge. They had potato pancakes instead of mashed potatoes. The garden, even in drought, had given them enough greens and carrots and beans and beets to feel like a feast. That year the tusenbladstårta had no cover of strawberries. Strawberries were too expensive in November.

The Third Threat Multiplier: Property Vulnerability

Farmers have been dealing with climate change since the invention of farming. That's what farming is: making as much food as possible with the weather you've been given. But cities, vastly more complex, do not adapt nearly as well to climate change. The world is full of history's once-great cities, abandoned to desert, subsumed by jungle, visited only by tourists.

Peter Sousounis is the director of climate change research at AIR Worldwide, where he works on catastrophe model development for large-scale clients, including insurance companies and reinsurers. He combines physics with actuarial data to provide the people who have the most at stake with the best answers on the climate future. The best estimate of the worldwide property damage due to sea level rise alone in the immediate future totals $1 trillion. But that only takes into account slow, steady rises in the sea level. The increase in unpredictability of extreme weather events means that much more than a mere $1 trillion is at risk. Over forty years, Category 5 hurricanes have increased by 300 percent globally. The direction is the same in all models, but the scale varies. "People have this ideal perception that climate change is happening slowly and steadily. In the grand scheme of things, it's not. It has fits and starts. It might even change direction temporarily," Sousounis says. "But I wholeheartedly believe that it will manifest itself nonlinearly rather than linearly. And that's what we have to be careful of. We need to account for nonlinearity." ("Nonlinearity" means that everything goes along as it always has until suddenly it doesn't.)

The models of the United Nations and the insurance companies are hedged bets. There are hundreds of climate models and they take the mean. But that conclusion is not the same as the result. In Vegas, if you're playing baccarat, in theory you should always come out even. It's a 50-50 bet. But you don't play baccarat to get your money back. The destructive total of climate change, for Sousounis, "could be, not to scare you, but 200 percent on the high side"—that is to say, 200 percent worse than the current standard model. If massive pieces of glaciers collapse, sudden sea level rise will follow, and with sudden sea level rise, the complex cascading system will spiral out of control. For Sousounis's clients, the increase in risk has one obvious consequence: "Definitely parts of the shoreline will be uninsurable."

We are inside a climate bubble. Bubbles pop. "The one thing there is reasonable consensus on, at least for hurricane activity, for the US, is overall an increase in the frequency and intensity of Category 4 or Category 5 hurricanes," Sousounis says. That fact alone is going to change America.

Nonlinear Climate Change

"New York would be incredibly high on the list of vulnerable cities," notes Vivek Shandas, director of the Institute for Sustainable Solutions at Portland State University in Portland, Oregon. The

Institute for Sustainable Solutions deals with the way cities will adapt to climate change. Some of the infrastructure in cities on the Eastern Seaboard dates from the eighteenth century, a disaster waiting to happen even before the compounding effect of multiple vulnerabilities from climate change. "Much of New York is relatively flat. Even modest levels of sea level rise are billions of dollars of infrastructure impact, and the available space to move is more concentrated as well," Shandas says. "Then you have heat waves that occur. We see deaths every year. Then there's urban flooding, because you have storm and sewer systems that are relatively outdated." Miami will see intense heat waves, sea level rise, and hurricanes happening at the same time. But Miami is just a great town. New York is New York; 88.3 percent of the world's foreign exchange pours through it.

Superstorm Sandy in 2012 was a warning shot. Across New York State, $32.8 billion was required for restoration. For a storm that was not technically even a hurricane when it hit New York, Sandy wrecked eight tunnels and stranded millions of commuters between Brooklyn and Lower Manhattan. New Jersey transit was shut down for nearly a month. The South Ferry subway station flooded with 15 million gallons of salt water and only resumed service in 2017. To repair and improve the subway, the Metropolitan Transportation Authority spent $4.5 billion. They are preparing for large storms by making it possible to seal terminals with retractable stairwell covers and other flood protection measures, including "flex gates," waterproof Kevlar belts to be unrolled, and "resilient tunnel plugs"—air balloons. But they can only prepare for what they know and for what they might expect. What would a Category 5 storm with an extra half a foot of sea surge do?

The Cascading Failure of Urban Systems

City failure happens incrementally and then by cataclysms. "The incremental failures are often things like the sewer systems can no longer handle the water coming in and the investment in the sewer system is no longer what the city can handle," Shandas says. "What failure means is a cascading failure of systems." It's a feedback loop. When population declines, the tax base declines. When the tax base declines, funding to deal with mitigation and adaptation declines, which leads to infrastructure breakdown, which leads to the inability to provide services, which leads to a population decline. "How much energy would a city need to continue sustaining itself?" Shandas asks. "How much do we want to keep subsidizing the activities within cities to keep them going? When do we say enough is enough? When can we no longer do it? What we haven't had a serious conversation about is managed retreat." Instead, the most likely scenario is that those with enough resources will flee, leaving behind the poor and vulnerable. The markets will respond after the crises without any mitigation of human costs. This is already happening in some places. Mexican Americans live on polluted areas that are totally unprotected near the Rio Grande. In 2020, California banned insurance companies from dropping homeowners' policies, a step to protect ordinary homeowners. But it means that nothing will stop people from continuing to build houses in unfeasible locations. The state will not take action on climate change, and they are preventing the market from taking action.

Eventually, climate change will force adaptation. Without the political will for investment—and remember that nobody ever got elected preventing a catastrophe—the forces driving managed retreat will be market forces. Insurance companies will tell home-owners they can no longer insure their properties. Those properties will lose their value because they can't be insured. Developers will build in safe areas because that will be the only real estate that holds its value. Some researchers in the field describe the effect as "climate gentrification"—tighter labor markets, increased prop-erty values where property survives, and more inequality. The rich will be able to afford the security of safe places, and the poor will live on the margins, in the darkness on the edge of town.

A marketplace retreat will produce a Fortress America, an America of walls, an America to keep out the sea, an America to keep out foreigners, an America to keep out the poor. Stable real estate will require more investment to maintain. "Then you have these massive events like Hurricane Maria in Puerto Rico, short-term and incredibly intense events that wipe out populations," Shandas says. This is a model well known to ecologists. It's how species go extinct.

The Crossing

Alone in her Gowanus apartment, the Producer is waiting for the event. Thirty-six hours before landfall, the NOAA upgrades Mu-riel to Category 2. Everybody receives the message on their devices simultaneously, a faint buzzing over the whole of New York. The Governor now implores the people of the city to evacuate. "If you can leave, leave. If you must stay, know what you're getting into. Muriel is going to pick up a good chunk of the Atlantic Ocean and dump it on us. Winds are going to reach 110 miles per hour." Most New Yorkers hear only that the storm was Category 2. Everybody knows that the wall can withstand up to Category 3.

The Producer listens to the Governor's warning but doesn't

consider leaving. She has a story to make. To her relief, the tenants in every other unit evacuate. They have to force their way across the bridges. All twenty-one bridges fill with last-minute evacuees. The tunnels have already flooded.

Then the storm surge comes. In Brooklyn, the surge rises from the canal, the tide drifting from the northwest, bringing with it the detritus from the surrounding houses and businesses, a flood

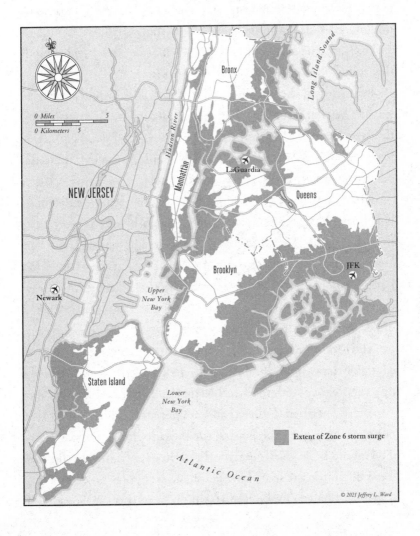

of books and papers, art and the displays from the Whole Foods on Gowanus. Several witnesses report seeing a baby floating in a stroller. Others remember a kind of foam of vegetables on the surface. Something, someone, had failed.

Within a few hours, the tidal surge floods JFK and LaGuardia airports. The power goes off for Manhattan and Staten Island at 8:37 p.m. By 9:45, power cuts out for most of the outlying boroughs. Red Hook, the most vulnerable New York neighborhood, no longer exists. In downtown Manhattan, Greenwich Village, Tribeca, and the East Village flood. Wall Street floods. The winds that follow the surge reach 116 miles per hour.

From Iowa, the Producer's husband calls, imploring her to leave. The chance to leave has passed. She will need to wait until the first effects of Muriel subside. She spends several days inside, in fear. The Governor calls the National Guard. A hundred thousand soldiers are making their way into the city.

After a few days, more out of curiosity than fear, the Producer half floats, half swims through the flotsam-blanketed seep over Fourth Avenue. The water has receded enough to walk there. She heads up the hill to Prospect Park. Prospect Park isn't Prospect Park anymore. The trees have tumbled. Whole families are curled up inside the sweep of horizontal branches. People are sleeping under the bushes, in a daze of upended lives.

The Producer heads back to her apartment. She didn't take out enough extra cash, she realizes. She barely has a few thousand. She fills a duffel bag with food and water and batteries. She tucks her Glock into her belt. Other than her chargers and her phone, she needs nothing else. She goes to the safe to remove the passports. The family Bible is in there, too, brought over from the old country. The thing's the size of her chest and weighs as much as a load of bricks. She can't take it. She can't bear to leave it. So she tells herself she'll come back. Her daughter's violin in the corner of the room, the furniture, the framed doll's dresses, the candlesticks she and her husband received as a wedding gift—she tells herself she'll be back for all of it.

Wading back onto Fourth Avenue, she joins in with the stream of other refugees along the old route to JFK. She's glad to have her Glock. A few hours down the road, the crowd of refugees slowly starts to thicken. She overhears rumors that the storm had been bigger than Category 3. Up ahead she can see groups standing, unsure what to do, where to go. The road has slopped into the water.

It's almost beautiful, the way the arch of the highway's concrete dips into the black waves. It reminds her of a Mayan ruin she once visited in Belize, a grand center of trade fifteen hundred years earlier, fitted with glamorous temples, now overrun by jungle. Here, for the first time, she asks herself: Did New York survive? What happened to the city she loved?

Boats of all types offer transport across the water: fishing vessels come down from New England, pleasure craft from the Jersey Shore, skiffs and motorboats that probably shouldn't be on open water. The new shoreline is abuzz with negotiation. Most of the transporters start at five grand a seat. But some of the heavier, safer craft go for ten, and the motorboats for as low as two. Most of the refugees, like the Producer, have little or no cash. Some of the deals are barter, for trade. The Producer watches a young couple, sitting on a cooler, pooling their jewelry, wedding rings and all. Other transporters can process credit cards on their phones. A gentlemanly fifty-year-old strides onto one of the larger skiffs, tapping his phone, as if paying for a latte at Starbucks.

The Producer realizes at that moment that she's a refugee. She's a refugee in her own country. They're all refugees in their own country, all these strangers on the new New York shoreline. How did Americans become refugees in their own country? What brought them to this?

On the other side of the waters, the army is loading the refugees into buses. On the bus to Iowa, the Producer finds she can tell who's a New Yorker and who's an Iowan. She always believed, when she lived in New York, that she could tell Midwesterners from locals. Now she knows she can. The New Yorkers look scared. The Iowans look bored.

The Imminent Crisis of Climate Change Refugees

The current best estimate for the future number of climate refugees from coastal areas is 13 million. Using historical patterns and machine learning to connect direct and indirect effects of climate change, a team of computer scientists and demographers working at multiple universities in 2020 came up with this model (see map on page 143), which is based entirely on sea level rise and no other environmental affect. The darker the square, the more refugees will be arriving.

The View from Climate Change Refugees

Climate change is already reshaping the United States. It is already upending people's lives. For decades, John Toto's family owned a traditional Italian family restaurant, Joe and John Toto's, across from Midland Beach in the Ocean Breeze neighborhood on Staten Island. The family lived across the street. During Sandy, Toto left when the water reached his knees; the restaurant had unmoored from its foundations by then. Sections of sidewalk had crumbled.

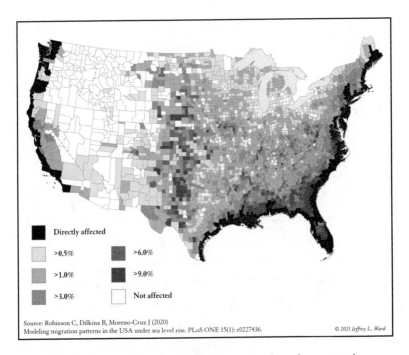

Source: Robinson C, Dilkina B, Moreno-Cruz J (2020)
Modeling migration patterns in the USA under sea level rise. PLoS ONE 15(1): e0227436.   © 2021 Jeffrey L. Ward

The Producer will be one of those dots moving from the coast to the center as the sea level rises.

"My house got pushed two hundred feet off the foundation," he remembers. "It was like *The Wizard of Oz*. My entire existence got turned upside down."

Ocean Breeze and Oakwood Beach were declared eligible for state buyouts at pre-storm values. New York bought six hundred homes. Federal flood insurance for houses damaged by Sandy has risen by as much as 25 percent. The area around the restaurant is gap-toothed. Toto points out the houses of some residents who were underwater on their mortgages before their houses went literally underwater. Since Sandy, Toto sold the restaurant to new owners who are turning the place into a barbecue joint. Some who can't afford to leave, or who are too old to start over, have stayed. Their new houses stand on stilts. One structure, an attached unit, has one intact, inhabited side and one crumbling, abandoned side. "It's a mixed bag," Toto says. The Ocean Breeze neighborhood was originally a salt marsh and never should have been built on. The land is returning to nature.

On the deck of the new place, Toto has left a painting on the wall, a mural of the waves at the height the waters reached during Hurricane Sandy. It hangs about level with your shoulders if you're sitting down. You can have a lovely meal, Staten Island barbecue, and see right where the water will rise to. "I wanted them to put that there as a reminder," Toto says. "People have no clue what this experience is. I do. And I do think it will happen again." Everybody knows it will happen again. They're still eating there.

Toto came back to Staten Island to rebuild because of massive investment by the state. It's unclear whether that would be possible after a massive outflow of its population. A different possible response to climate change catastrophe followed the Camp Fire conflagration in Paradise, California. Fifty-two thousand people evacuated. Only half of them ended up staying in California. The wealthier people moved to the nearby town of Chico. On the Facebook group Camp Fire survivors use to share their stories and to stay in touch, they have registered their presence in forty-eight states. They've also left records of the randomness of their lives:

I find myself in Washington with no family around. And life is still hard. But I'm working on it. I finally found a job, I got a travel trailer. I made it work but yes we are still struggling and we might be for a while but will be okay. Me and my kids miss our lives but there's nothing we can do about it. We miss our family, we miss our friends, we miss our home, and we miss our stuff. I still haven't went to counseling like my mom said I should but I think I might need it. Because I find myself crying over the littlest things. We are strong, I just keep telling myself at least we're alive.

I've arrived at Murphy, North Carolina now, staying at an air B and B rental cabin here. It's the first chapter in a new adventure to have moved across the US at 66, disabled and knowing NO one here where I've moved. Now to find a new long-term home—fingers crossed!

I am now in a new state, in a beautiful town. Everyone here is so nice, and I have a new home as well. I know I should just feel lucky to be alive, but something inside me died that day and cannot be recovered. I miss my pets, my home, and my neighbors and it sickens me that some did not make it. I dream each night of my pets who died and the idea of their suffering terrifies me. I cannot eat or sleep normally now; nothing brings me pleasure anymore. I am bereft. I cannot abide the death of my community.

I have decided to give myself one year, until November 8th, 2019, to see if anything will change. Sometimes I wish that I too had died that day.

After Hurricane Katrina, around 100,000 citizens were trapped in New Orleans. That disastrous evacuation—a case study in emergency mismanagement—resulted in several hundred deaths by heat and dehydration within a few days. Eventually, 1,800 died there; 1.36 million applied for assistance. The scale of human de-struction for a hurricane hitting New York would be exponentially greater.

The Politics of Climate Change Refugees

Robert McLeman studies migration patterns and climate change at Wilfrid Laurier University in Waterloo, Ontario. He has a dis-armingly cheerful, upbeat way of describing the spread of total pandemonium. Climate change can bring about political chaos, in large part through migration. The rise of temperature or sea level won't necessarily break people. It's what you don't expect that breaks you. I'm Canadian, so no cold snap, no snow dump, can break me. I'm used to it. I know what to do. But I wouldn't know what to do in the case of even a mild drought. Bangladesh, to take an example, will typically not experience mass migration due to flooding, because people in that region have been dealing with floods for thousands of years. But a drought could cause a serious crisis, causing waves of migration into India that result in political chaos.

What could Americans adapt to? And what could break them? Most worrying to McLeman is the fact that American populations are growing in the areas that are most vulnerable to unpredictable catastrophes. They include coastal New York, coastal New Jersey, Florida, coastal Louisiana, the Carolinas, the Valley of the Sun, the Bay Area, and Los Angeles. Many Central Americans who were separated from their children at the American border were fleeing gangs and political instability, but they were also fleeing drought. "Environmentally related migration already happens; we're just seeing the thin edge of the wedge right now," McLeman says.

You cannot read a history of fascism that does not attribute its popularity, in part, to the deeper trends of the Great Depression. A 2012 study from the National Bureau of Economic Research confirmed "the existence of a link between political extremism and economic hard times as captured by growth or contraction of the economy." The future of America will involve severe drought, economic downturn, and the erosion of major coastal cities. The political scenarios in the previous two reports reveal the dangers of these realities. The rise of the hard right and hyper-partisan Washington emerged, tangentially, from the collapse of the housing market in 2008. The rising chaos works both ways. American institutions respond weakly to emergencies. The emergencies weaken the American institutions, which, in turn, diminish their capacity to respond to emergencies. It's a cycle. American families are chewed up.

No policy solutions, not even the most extreme, would prevent what I have described here.

The Thanksgiving After the Fall of New York

The Producer didn't travel home for Thanksgiving that year. She was already there. Months after the fall of New York, there's no longer reliable data on suicide rates or food insecurity. There are large drifting groups of human wreckage exploding in random violence or moving away from fear and toward the hope of safety. For the Producer, the relief of escape and reunion have passed. Vanished New York is worse than a wound to her. It's a cauterized future. It's a closed escape hatch while the waters are rising. The Producer fought so hard to break out of Iowa, to climb her way to the center of the world. And then the center of the world disappeared. She had some amazing audio footage of her escape from New York in the end. There was no one to sell it to.

At first, no one doubted that they would rebuild New York. Everybody talked about "New York tough," and writers published pieces written about the surprising joys of having to take the Brooklyn Ferry again, and sidewalk vendors hawked FUCK YOU, MURIEL, YOU BITCH T-shirts outside the World Trade Center. After the Second World War, Germany and Japan rebuilt Berlin and Tokyo. After the earthquake of 1755, the Portuguese rebuilt Lisbon. But in all those cases, they assumed that their cities would not face such an uncertain future. If New York is forever more vulnerable to hurricanes, why rebuild it? *How* to rebuild it? The city and state and the federal government face an insuperable challenge, tasked with the almost incalculable cost of rebuilding the bulk of New York City's infrastructure for an unpredictable future. And how could they raise the money when the people have fled? Who was going to pay the taxes?

The Producer's husband has moved back to New York by then, and crossing the country is too much, even for Thanksgiving. He's part of a salvage crew in the Bronx, digging up the abandoned subways for precious metals. All that devastated infrastructure has become the richest scrap metal in the world.

As for her nephew, he vanished one morning, leaving a note: He went to look for his father in North Dakota. When he bought a phone, he would call them. That's what the note said.

His mother took his note seriously. She had to. But the Producer knew better. Her nephew had become one of the untraceable, the phoneless. He could have joined anyone. The Dakota Gadsdens. The local branch of the Atomwaffen Division. One of the separatist communes forming across the country. Or just one of the roving gangs. Still, they left his room exactly as he had left it, plastered with the historical Nazi and Allied propaganda, vintage images of *Sharknado* and *Dawn of the Dead*, the ceiling with dangling models of bombers.

At least they still have the garden. The Producer and her sister built an electric fence around the edges of the property after a few thieves snuck in, looking for marijuana and chickens. She was glad she'd brought the Glock with her from the city, but she bought a couple of Mossberg pump-action shotguns too.

As she sets the table for the family in the long dining room, the Producer finds herself recalling the Thanksgiving her cousin Rose returned from the Iraq War back in the early 2000s, the cackle of her mother's laughter in the kitchen, her uncle and her dad in the hubbub of some argument, who can remember about what. All those happy memories are burdened with the sense of defeat now. Is it just the passing of time? Nobody's life goes the way it's supposed to go. Everybody knows the numbing sting of what might have been. She thought she would have grown into maturity by now, into security, into property, into control over her own life, a legacy to offer the future, if only some wisdom.

At the Big House, the sisters live in the shadow of their mother's exhaustion. They know, with a shared sense of guilt they don't have to acknowledge, that their own stalled lives have burdened their mother. They should be inviting her to Thanksgiving at one of their houses. But they'll never own anything.

The food this Thanksgiving is a little better. Not enough for leftovers but plenty for now. They have turkey again, and mashed potatoes with real butter. The garden did well with a little more rain. They made beans with slivered almonds and carrots and beets and sweet potatoes and shredded cabbage. The whole family gathers around as it always had. Everybody agrees that rice stuffing with sage tastes better than bread stuffing.

What happened? The Producer won't know as she looks back, trying to figure it out. The systems that keep us alive are ghostly, invisible. When they're gone, we won't even be able to say with any certainty what we've lost. She will sometimes blame herself and sometimes blame her times, and she'll be right both ways. She, like her country, has stumbled from crisis to crisis. And the hardest fact is that the catastrophes they've lived through—the crash, the drought, the fall of New York—are only preludes. Worse is to come. They remain the lucky ones—for now.

THE OUTBREAK OF WIDESPREAD VIOLENCE

You'll see it in on your feed, or maybe you'll be out and catch it on a television in the corner of a coffee shop, or somebody you love will call or text. Everyone's phones will go off at once. In your office, on the street, on the screen, horrified spectators, stopped still, with their hands to their mouths, gasping, running in vague panic. Smoke lifting over the Capitol—gray and black fumes billowing from the top of the great dome. A dirty bomb at the heart of power.

The photographs will be unforgettable: the horrifying cloud visible from Arlington cemetery, the burning mirrored in the Reflecting Pool in front of the Lincoln Memorial, a casual shot from the East Potomac Golf Course of players teeing off while the government burns behind them. Even before anyone knows who committed the atrocity, the news will report that everything has changed, that America will never be the same.

The news will be right. Everything will have changed. America is one spectacular act of political violence away from a national crisis.

The Power of the Gesture

Only a spark is needed, one major domestic terrorist event that shifts the perception of the country—an anti-government patriot who takes his rage against federal authority and finds expression in a drone loaded with explosives flown into the Capitol dome. The politics of the terrorist and even the violence itself won't matter so much as the shock the violence produces, the perception it conjures.

Even a small gesture can completely alter the public's consciousness of its own security. In 1970, in my own country, Canada, a separatist splinter group kidnapped a Quebec cabinet minister and a British diplomat. That was enough for the prime minister, Pierre Trudeau, an icon of liberalism, to declare martial law and suspend civil liberties. The kidnappings were, in themselves, of very limited moment or importance. The threat to the stability of government was negligible. The separatist party in question, the Front de libération du Québec, was disorganized and minor. It didn't matter. It was a question of perception: when the country felt out of control, the government had to respond.

That sense of control has already frayed in America. On January 6, 2020, rioters beat a policeman to death on the steps of the Capitol, smeared feces on the walls, took selfies in the House chamber, and stole souvenirs. The event was widely described as an insurrection. It wasn't. The rioters were only loosely organized and possessed little political support and no military support. But those facts may easily change. What will it be like when they come back shooting? The riot of January 6 should be taken as evidence of how political partisans will treat the onset of violence: 45 percent of Republican voters support the assault on Washington. "There's a lot of people out there calling for the end of violence . . . ," Rush Limbaugh said on his show the day after. "I am glad Sam Adams, Thomas Paine, the actual Tea Party guys, the men at Lexington and Concord, didn't feel that way." As January 6 has faded from the news, Republican talking points have continued to diminish its importance. "Watching the TV footage of those who entered the Capitol and walked through Statuary Hall showed people in an orderly fashion staying between the stanchions and ropes taking videos and pictures," Georgia Republican Andrew Clyde said in

May. "You know, if you didn't know the TV footage was a video from January the 6th, you would actually think it was a normal tourist visit." The representative was signaling. The Republican Party has become a movement with a political and an armed wing; the connection is clarifying. The relationship between the two is rarely direct—as in the case of the Oregon state representative literally opening the door for rioters. It's more often expressed laterally, sometimes through gestures, like Senator Josh Hawley's raised fist in support of the rioters, and sometimes through legislation, like the new restrictions on voting that continue to cast doubt, peripherally, on the legitimacy of the 2020 election. Meanwhile, the impotence of the government only becomes more naked: the greatest deliberative body in the world cannot manage to investigate an assault on its own members.

The question of civil war is only a matter of scale. All it would take is for the violence that's already manifested—the LA riots in 1992; the defiance of the federal authority by Arkansas in 1957; the sagebrush rebels shooting federal authorities as they have in recent years; the January 6 storming of the Capitol; white power groups promoting lone-wolf terrorism as they do—to fuse, through the rage-fueled mechanisms of the internet, into widespread conflict after a cataclysmic event. In hindsight, the cataclysmic event will appear completely natural, a logical outcome to the trends of the country.

The United States is particularly vulnerable to terrorist spectacle. September 11 was an act of significant destruction, but its iconic status, the meaning it took on in the American consciousness, was outsized. The resonance of September 11 in public life caused the United States to enter two failed wars and to continue those wars long after any national or global interests were being served. A domestic September 11 would create the same irresistible momentum. A serious assault on the political symbols, a sense that the nation, as a body, could be under threat, would inevitably provoke the impetus for revenge and the hunger for order.

The United States would not respond rationally to an assault on the Capitol. It would not manage to find a considered policy broadly supportive of the goal of restoring peace to the country and reducing tensions within its sectarian fronts. The underlying tensions in the country are too strong, the sense of threat too developed. If history is any guide, the reaction would be oversized. It would be violent. It would be controlling. It would be vengeful.

How Close America Has Come

In two separate incidents in the past fifteen years, radical right-wing partisans with violent intentions had access to low-grade nuclear weapons. They were discovered by accident. The first was in Maine. "On 9 December 2008, radiological dispersal device components and literature, and radioactive materials, were discovered at the Maine residence of an identified deceased James Cummings," the *Bangor Daily News* reported. The second was in Florida. In 2017, one of the roommates of a National Guardsman named Brandon Russell shot two of his other roommates. In their shared property, police found a cooler filled with HMTD, a high-power explosive, along with thorium and americium, both nuclear fuels. Russell had Atomwaffen ties. Cummings was a white supremacist. Both Cummings and Russell were caught by accident, not by anti-terrorism efforts. Cummings's wife shot him. One of Russell's roommates shot the others. Those peripheral crimes, not efforts by law enforcement, led to the uncovering of the nuclear materials. How many other Cummingses and Russells are out there right now?

What a Dirty Bomb Does

"The effects from radiation exposure would likely be minimal," a Department of Homeland Security report on the effects of dirty bombs makes clear. The spectacle is the main problem. "Psychological effects from fear of being exposed may be one of the major consequences of a dirty bomb." A dirty bomb at the Capitol building would serve as an act of annihilating symbolism more than an act of physical destruction. But that wouldn't diminish its power. "Such impacts might involve disruption to lives and livelihoods as the contaminated area is being cleaned up," the DHS report adds. This impact could continue even after the site has been cleaned up if people are reluctant to return to the affected area." The disruption of the legislative body would devastate the country's faith in its capacity to negotiate solutions peacefully.

How the Country Changes

At first you won't necessarily notice much of a change. Violence has always defined America. There have always been two sides to every story. The *New York Times* and MSNBC will begin by blaming the catastrophe on the Secret Service and the FBI, who, in their view, have shirked the threat from domestic terrorism for too long. Fox News and the rest of the conservative media will bemoan the rising incivility in American politics. Online discourse will be rife with conspiracy theories. Anyone who can be blamed will be blamed—the Jews, the Muslims, immigrants. "White democracy eats itself," the radicals on the left will claim. Others will be happy, or will claim they are happy, now that the facade of democracy has been stripped away. White power groups will claim that it's all a false flag and that the long-awaited race war is finally underway. All of this already happens after acts of political violence in the United States today.

To clamp down on domestic terrorism, the US government will have no choice but to control arms, control the movement of people, and control hate speech. Even the first of these requirements will be technically unfeasible and counterproductive. A significant portion of the US population considers any attempt to curtail, or even to register, the private possession of military-grade weapons inherently un-American. How much more un-American will they consider limits on movement and speech? The American government, in order to survive, will have to suspend the most sacred icon of the American government, the Bill of Rights. So, right from the beginning, as an inevitable element of this kind of war, a massive portion of the US populace, nearly half, would consider the actions of the US government un-American. And they wouldn't be wrong.

The United States has been involved in counterinsurgency conflicts for over fifty years. It has never learned enough to avoid the first trap: the violence that imposes order to control violence produces more violence and more disorder. The means of counterinsurgency are in direct conflict with their ends: You cannot reach pacification by murdering people. Over and over again, the methods of control generate chaos.

American Counterinsurgency Strategy

Fortunately, or unfortunately, we have a pretty good idea of how the United States government would respond to an outbreak of mass political violence. After decades of failure, the American military has a complete manual on the subject: *Joint Publication 3-24, Counterinsurgency*, or *JP 3-24*.

There are two basic strategies at work in current military policy around counterinsurgency: they go by the acronyms SCHBT and ISIR. SCHBT stands for "Shape, Clear, Hold, Build, Transition," mentioned earlier, and ISIR for "Identify, Separate, Influence, Renunciation." Ultimately these are not that different from the "oil slick strategy" used during the Algerian War of Independence. The military holds areas of loyalty and moves outward from them. The first requirement is to determine areas of loyalty. During the desegregation crisis in Arkansas, Eisenhower's first order was to hold the Arkansas National Guard to barracks. He didn't want to test their loyalty. A military force would move from, say, Portland, where the belief in government legitimacy is comparatively strong, county by county, into rural Oregon, which is rife with anti-government patriotism.

ISIR is a strategy for de-radicalizing youth in the areas under control. How do you de-radicalize youth while at the same time taking away their most basic rights? You can't. It's hard to find youth so stupid that you can kill and imprison their parents and tell them you love them afterward. It didn't work in Iraq and Afghanistan. It won't work in the United States.

JP 3-24 is the culmination of decades of failure. It's a manual born out of lost wars. Because it has been written by those who need to articulate some kind of operational purpose, it imagines the possibility of victory. But those who have fought in America's counterinsurgencies have suffered enough to abandon false hopes just because they serve an institutional purpose. Not that there aren't differences of opinion. While some veteran officers insist that counterinsurgency can never succeed, others believe that, under specific conditions and with clear limits, counterinsurgency can achieve a few, narrow goals.

Daniel Bolger, a retired lieutenant general and history professor at North Carolina State University, is the author of *Why We Lost*, an on-the-ground report on the failures of two decades of American counterinsurgency. Bolger studied counterinsurgency in military school and even wrote a speculative novel about the Afghan war of the late 1980s from the Russian perspective. When he found himself as part of an occupying force in Jalalabad, he knew, perhaps as much as anyone could know, the folly of occupation. "It is a militarily futile and stupid thing to engage in. Most countries regret it," he says. "You can go back to Roman times, to ancient China. Whenever you get into these situations, it tends to bleed the occupiers." His view about the counterinsurgency manuals is definite. "Most of this stuff is just bunk. We're kidding ourselves if we think this stuff is going to work. There's a flawed assumption at the base of the counterinsurgency field manual. If we, as outsiders, are going to secure the population, we are already wrong. How can we do that as outsiders?" The false premise of counterinsurgency is that you can change the minds of people through force. Wars of counterinsurgency are wars of perception. You can't murder your way to any perception other than that you're a murderer.

It's in the nature of insurgent conflict that violence builds on itself. Symbolic horrors echo. Resonance compounds. The most recent counterinsurgency manual, *JP 3-24*, has digested, or at least acknowledged, the problem of perception. Insurgencies and counterinsurgencies are engaged in competitive storytelling. "Insurgent groups harness narratives to communicate grievances, goals, and justifications for actions to both internal and external audiences," *JP 3-24* reads. "Insurgency narratives have three elements or components: actors and the environments in which they operate, events along a temporal continuum, and causality—cause and effect relative to the first two elements." The key word here is "audiences." And how good can any military force be at playing to audiences?

The Spectacular Nature of Twenty-First-Century Conflict

You will be the audience. You yourself will be the battleground of the conflict. The war is over your feelings about the war. You will begin on one side or the other. Stories will accumulate. Soldiers will fill the street. Flags will hang out of windows. You will feel that the other side is all terrorists and they will feel that you are a terrorist. As they already do.

At first, the horrors will seem distant. You will talk about them with your friends. The military brings in tanks to crush a pocket of apocalyptic cultists who are preparing for armed resistance. Was it overreach? Sovereign citizens, organized in posses, stalk Chicago and the cities of the Northwest murdering protestors. Should there be armed left-wing groups to respond? The statehouse impeaches a Southern governor for hate speech after he critiques the Democratic president. What about the First Amendment, or should that be suspended? An attempt to disarm Oregon Three Percenters after they hang a government informant turns into a bloodbath on both sides. Running gun battles erupt over the rights to herd cattle on federal lands in the West. Racialized terrorism becomes as normal as mass shootings in the United States currently are. The government declares martial law and suspends the writ of habeas corpus.

The number of places you visit will shrink. Where is safe? *Who* is safe? Control and chaos feed into each other and feed into despair. When you see an officer of the law, you ask yourself: *Which side is he on?* Public spaces in general are dangerous. You can't go to a movie without wondering who's going to shoot it up. Fracture means threat.

You will know how you feel about all of this. The more confusing America gets, the more clear everyone will believe it to be. As your side commits evil, you will become entrenched. There must have been an even greater evil to justify it.

The Importance of the Military Oath

Who controls the military is the most important question. The US military is a true transnational institution. In 2017, a Gallup poll found that Americans' trust in the military is double that of the presidency and six times that of Congress. The worship of the armed forces has been ingrained into ordinary American life since the beginning of the Iraq War. No sporting event can happen in the US without a celebration of a member of the military. Many airlines give the military priority boarding on US flights. Some grocery stores offer preferred parking to military families. The US military occupies 2 percent of all federal land in the continental United States. Its economic activity constitutes 3.1 percent of the GDP. There are nearly 20 million veterans. Worried analysts in the military describe an emerging "monopoly of trust," a position of reverence they don't want. The military functions as a tool. That is how it sees itself. It is not supposed to be in charge. Soldiers would serve a constitutionally elected government whether they considered it legitimate or not. Right-wing infiltration into the military is less of a concern than partisan infiltration into law enforcement, because the oath and the chain of command are clear.

A coup would hardly be unprecedented in global terms: in

Chile, in 1973, a constitutional democracy in place for forty-five years devolved into winner-take-all, zero-sum partisan politics until the military imposed *tranquilidad*. Other countries, even established democracies like Canada, have imposed martial law in the middle of severe political upheaval. But a hard coup in the United States—tanks rolling up Pennsylvania Avenue to impose military control over the country—is unlikely. The deep-seated causes of almost every coup, anywhere, are "poverty, economic activities based mostly on land, and hybrid political regimes," according to Taeko Hiroi, a professor at the University of Texas at El Paso who studies the causes and triggers of coups. Countries which are neither authoritarian nor democratic are most vulnerable. The immediate triggers of coups tend to be "social instability, anti-government protests, economic crisis and regime transitions." It's not that these conditions are inconceivable for the United States, but the real reason why a hard coup is unlikely is simply that it hasn't happened before. "One of the most important factors in a country's propensity to experience coups is its history," Hiroi says. "Coups are more likely to happen to countries that have experienced coups."

The Situation at the Outbreak

Both the right and the left have structural advantages. The right will benefit from the ferocity and militarization of its base, significant infiltration of the radical right into institutional life, and the legacy of the Senate and the Electoral College. The left, for its part, makes up the majority of the country, and they have the money. Biden-voting counties in 2020 accounted for 70 percent of the national GDP. With each side's respective strengths, there will be no overwhelming force or clear winner from the outset.

The Impossible Solution

For Daniel Bolger, the problem of counterinsurgency is fundamentally not a military one: "A succession of winning firefights makes exactly no difference. The local people have to run their own government." When you read Bolger's book *Why We Lost*, you keep waiting for the losses. The Americans win nearly every engagement, and totally. They have excellent plans that are well-executed. Their collection of victories is irrelevant. "By definition, you're the occupier, and everything you do just proves to the local population that their 'local government' is nothing but a proxy or a tool," he says. It's the classic case of if you lose, you lose, and if you win, you still lose.

The tactical considerations of battles between the military and the militia forces on United States would be completely irrelevant. No one with any tactical expertise can imagine anything other than a one-sided engagement. Professional military forces are professional. No one with any political expertise in counterinsurgency could imagine that any of those victories would matter. Rather, every time the Marines demolished another outpost of resistance, it would only exacerbate the underlying crises.

In Dispatch One, I outlined what an engagement between the US military and anti-government patriots might look like. In the opinion of every military expert I talked to, there was no question of who would win the battle. But the United States has lost a series of wars in which it has won the vast majority of engagements. "You will occasionally hear people say, 'I'm not worried about an insurrection because the army's got all the tanks and the air force has bombers,'" Bolger says. "Look, if that's what you're reduced to, just going in and killing people, you're not solving the insurrection. In fact, you're spreading it. You're guaranteeing more of it." You cannot punish people out of hating you. The military is an instrument of punishment. Its very function makes it useless. For Bolger, who has seen this futility from every angle, counterinsurgency strategy is a contradiction in terms. It is a game in which the only winning strategy is not to play. But not everyone has the luxury of not playing.

Retired colonel Peter Mansoor has a different perspective. For Mansoor, a successful counterinsurgency is next to—but not quite—impossible, a vital distinction. For one thing, insurgencies fail when they are unpopular with the local population, as in the cases of the Shining Path in Peru and Che Guevara in Bolivia. "The most important thing is to get the politics right, and if you get the politics right, you're going to be able to win a counterinsurgency," Mansoor says, while acknowledging that "the reason these insurgencies occur in the first place is because of politics." The role of the military, in Mansoor's view, is to clamp down on violence so that political progress can be made. "If you have so much violence going on, the politics is frozen," he says. That need for stability to promote dialogue was the assumption behind the Surge in Iraq in 2007. And there, an expanded counterinsurgency strategy did make politics possible. It's just that the parties found themselves exactly where they started before the violence.

Ingrowing Despair

The solution to the next civil war will be the solution to the crises America already faces. The military at best could provide the space that the United States currently possesses to negotiate its problems. If America cannot solve these problems now, why would it be able to solve them after widespread violence?

Once counterinsurgency starts, it's nearly impossible to extricate your forces. How can anyone manage to maintain perspective in the middle of a fight for survival? "You get focused because it's life-or-death on patrols, ambushes, night raids, because your life is on the line," Bolger says. "You're hopeful, as you're doing that, that somebody way up the chain is thinking, 'Hey, I'm making these guys do this because this is getting us towards whatever we want.' My experience was that they were making us do it because that's what we did. I don't think they had an overall plan that I could detect. When you're talking about your own country, the stakes would be much higher."

JP 3-24 has a nifty graphic explaining how to win a counterinsurgency. It involves three neat political goals.

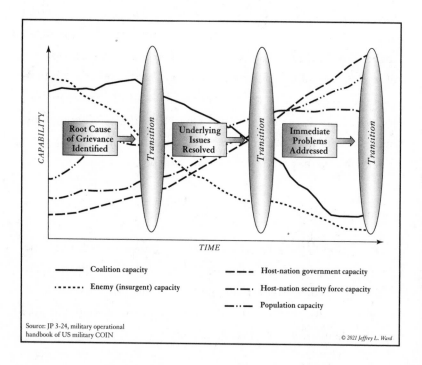

CAPABILITY

Root Cause of Grievance Identified

Transition

Underlying Issues Resolved

Transition

Immediate Problems Addressed

Transition

TIME

——— Coalition capacity   — — — Host-nation government capacity

· · · · · · · Enemy (insurgent) capacity   — · — · Host-nation security force capacity

                                                — · · — Population capacity

Source: JP 3-24, military operational
handbook of US military COIN

© 2021 Jeffrey L. Ward

Do I need to point out how impossible this is in the case of the United States? There are whole libraries devoted to identifying the root causes of American grievances. Addressing the country's immediate problems is increasingly beyond the capacity of the government no matter who forms it. And as for the "resolution of the underlying issues," what would such a question even mean? The resolution of a country devoted to liberty but founded on slavery? The resolution of a political order built on revolutionary overthrowing? How do you resolve the glorious contradictions of the Republic, the contradictions that have made it great? What would that even look like?

The Evanescence of Democracy

The stakes would keep rising, as every attempt to contain the violence would lead to more resistance, and the rising violence of the resistance would lead to more ferocious attempts to contain it. Mass shootings at military bases, which have already occurred, will spark retribution and more intense security strictures. Atrocities will blossom into brighter and brighter flames. The wealthy, in gated communities, will up the quantity and quality of their private security. The poor, as they do now, will fear gangs and join them. The machinery of American democracy will continue to function. The country will hold elections. Parties will change power. But they will increasingly matter less and less. Once the state gets involved in political violence, the machinery of the peaceful transition of power is superfluous. The insurgents will want political power. If you deny it to them, which must happen to preserve the state, its machinery is useless.

The Unlikelihood of a Hard Coup in the United States

One of the reasons that hard coups—militaries taking over civilian governments—have become so rare generally is that partisans the world over have found them increasingly unnecessary. "There are many different ways to remove the president," Taeko Hiroi points out. Impeachment is much quieter. The supporters of indicted presidents—in Brazil, in Israel—consider the transitions that overthrow their leaders "coups," but the mechanisms aren't extra-constitutional. "Soft coups" or "self-coups" are the preferred methods by which a sitting executive consolidates his or her power. (The term, in Spanish, is *autogolpe*.) In 1992, in Peru, democratically elected president Alberto Fujimori sent tanks to the legislature so he could reform the system to guarantee his own power. Neither Erdogan in Turkey nor Putin in Russia found the need. There is a way to walk the line: following constitutional procedures while ensuring that all the power concentrates in the hands of the executive.

A self-coup is well underway in America already. The rise of executive power is the rare case of a truly bipartisan trend. The use of executive legislation, bypassing Congress, began in earnest with Ronald Reagan, continued under Clinton, expanded under Bush, and became standard under Obama and Trump. What was once an exception made for cases of national emergency now goes unremarked.

The Prospect of Trying to Control the United States

For Mansoor, the sheer scale of the United States in terms of geography and population would present a massive military problem.

"You need a troop ratio where you have a lot of security forces to clamp down on violence. The United States is a very large continent with large population. I'm not sure we could ever have that many people in uniform to make it happen. What you would see is the rise of militias on both sides." The military's role will be to clamp down on violence. The only way to clamp down on violence would be to put the country on lockdown.

"You have to control the population," Mansoor says. "In Baghdad we did that by segmenting off the city with cement barriers, by instituting martial law and censuses. There was a curfew. There were checkpoints all over the place. We went into people's homes in cordon-and-search operations looking for arms and munitions. We had a full-scale intelligence operation to ferret out the terrorist and insurgent leaders. We had an unblinking eye over the city taking 24/7 surveillance. It's very invasive for civil rights. It became essentially impossible for the terrorists and insurgents to move or communicate." Areas of population were broken down by ethnicity and by twelve-foot, steel-reinforced blast walls. Citizens were interrogated every time they left or entered their neighborhoods. Anyone suspicious was arrested. "This is the other thing that would occur. Massive detention centers across the United States, where people who were suspected of being disloyal or who were disloyal would be warehoused on a massive scale," Mansoor adds. The United States is already the most incarcerated society in the world. A civil war would make it vastly more so.

An insurgent conflict in America, the only country in the world where there are more guns than people, would eclipse all previous insurgent conflicts. It is much more diverse than any other country in the world, with a hugely heterogeneous population. It exists in explicit resistance to state control.

The Cycle of Spectacular Violence and Repression

Spectacular violence isn't new to America. In 1867, the *New York Times* reported on a public fund set up in Colorado. "At a mass meeting held in one of the little towns in that Territory recently, a fund of $5,000 was subscribed for the purpose of buying Indian scalps, and $25 each is to be paid for scalps with the ears on. From this it would seem that the citizens of that delectable Territory cannot trust each other in a matter which they represent to be of such vital importance to themselves, and so require the ears to be produced with each scalp lest some dishonest cut-throat should make two out of one, and so obtain more than his share of blood money." If a second civil war comes to America, it will not lack for precedents of annihilating fury and indiscriminate murder.

The horrors of this kind of conflict are bottomless: the rage feeds on itself, the spectacle builds. In the Syrian civil war, government forces stuck heads on pikes to display their intent of total war. Insurgent resistance forces committed genocides against smaller tribes. Any international agreements about the Laws of War— the ban on chemical or biological weapons, say—meant nothing quickly. Torture became standard practice.

The use of torture is the ultimate folly of counterinsurgency. Whatever its uses in individual cases, which can be significant, torture has never been broadly effective. You cannot clamp down on violence by elaborating suffering. The French learned its corrupting seduction during the Algerian war of independence. Without torture, by almost all assessments, they would have lost the Battle of Algiers, and if they had lost the Battle of Algiers, they would have lost Algeria. But by their use of torture, they lost Algeria

anyway, and their own souls besides. Albert Camus had the clear-
est view of it: "Torture has perhaps saved some at the expense of
honour, by uncovering thirty bombs, but at the same time it has
created fifty new terrorists who, operating in some other way and
in another place, would cause the death of even more innocent people." Pierre-Henri Simon, a close observer, witnessed the deeper
futility of the whole process. By the use of torture, the policeman
"injures in himself the essence of humanity." But it is worse with
the military: "It is here that the honour of the nation becomes engaged." America is already engaged in torture, and has been for
generations. In 1999, the US Congress voted to close the United
States Army School of the Americas, acknowledging the atrocities
they had spawned.

How long could such repression last? "We're talking about a
future civil war in the United States, so the effort would extend
indefinitely because of the passions that would invoke," Mansoor
says. For Bolger, as a historian as well as a retired officer, what is
extraordinary is how little the United States has learned from even
the insurgencies on its own soil. The British Army won nearly
every pitched battle in the Revolutionary War. They could not hold
the country against the will of its inhabitants. "The United States
has had and has dealt with a significant amount of political violence from the beginning," he says. The Constitution is the document of a revolutionary people. Like the Yugoslavian and Algerian
constitutions, the document retains elements of its revolutionary
origins; the Second Amendment insists on the rights of militias. It
was written by militia men.

The failure of Reconstruction after the first Civil War reveals
the near impossibility of holding Americans under a political regime they won't tolerate. The North won the war but couldn't

stomach occupation. "What really happens? The Northern forces struggle, undergunned, undermanned, with provisional support from the government, a very small occupying force up to 1877, and every year everybody's looking at their watch saying 'Are we done yet?'" Bolger says. "So what happens? The African American population that's nominally free becomes peons with almost no rights by 1877, basically disenfranchised in every practical sense, and the people in the North accepted it because they knew they couldn't do anything about it. They weren't going to kill every single Southerner." The compromise of 1877 was ultimately the retreat of federal power. "The South got essentially home rule," Bolger says. Reconstruction was in a sense the first failed American occupation.

The Exhaustion

You won't recognize your own country. You won't recognize your own time. You'll still have a job. You'll go to work. You'll raise your kids. It will be possible, just, to cling to a sense of normalcy, although it is exactly normal life that becomes impossible. Your city will burn. Your hospitals will fill. Your police will take sides. You will have to have papers to go out and to go home. Your children will need papers to get into school. You will constantly be in contact with military personnel. Rights that you've taken for granted your entire life will be suspended. The stories will accumulate: ever-expanding factionalism, ever-deepening loathing, the stakes of the monstrous spectacles rising. You won't know what to believe after a while. All information will become propaganda. The news will fill with hate crimes, public lynchings, summary executions of right-wing figures in retaliation, urban riots that spill over, people dragged to their deaths behind trucks. When will you be one of the stories?

The De Facto End of the Union

To ordinary people, to Americans trying to live their lives caught between the random violence of terrorists and the grinding repression of the state, victory and defeat will look much the same. "If you're in a situation where you're using armed force to try and quell a population, you're either going to have to kill a bunch of them or you're going to pull out and let them have local control," Lieutenant General Bolger says. "You're never going to talk them into seeing it your way." The United States, as an entity, survived one civil war. The question for the next civil war is not necessarily whether the United States would survive but whether it would be recognizable afterward.

What Victory Would Mean

The typical conclusion of insurgency conflicts is not victory by either side but exhaustion by all. Exhaustion would reshape the American political landscape. "What bargains or deals would be struck with local authorities to stop the violence?" Bolger wonders. A devolution of power wouldn't even require any formal legislation. The transition could be quite surreptitious. It's a question of what laws the federal government would choose to enforce. There is precedence. Women in some states could vote fifty years before it was federal law. "Would what resulted look much like the America we know today?" Bolger asks. "I don't know. The question is at what point does it cause the society as a whole to fracture. At what point does it go too far, and you say 'Okay, this is no longer a country'? We're all just pretending it's the same thing." That question is not just for future Americans. It is impinging on the present. With or without a civil war, Americans are going to face an existential question: Are they the same country anymore? Or are they just pretending?

THE END OF THE REPUBLIC

One way or another, the United States is coming to an end. The divisions have become intractable. The political parties are irreconcilable. The capacity for government to make policy is diminishing. The icons of national unity are losing their power to represent. The threat multipliers from economic and environmental sources are driving an underlying tribalism that is shredding the ability of the political order to respond to threats against its own stability. The Constitution is becoming incoherent.

One possible conclusion is violence. The other is civilized separation. At this point, disunion is among the best-case scenarios for the United States.

Secession as a Possibility

Secession would not be a failure, given the tensions tearing the United States apart. Separatism is a worldwide political trend. The number of states in the world has tripled since 1945. And there will soon be more. "Right now, there are about sixty secessionist movements worldwide. Sixty independence movements is a pretty large number by historical standards," says Ryan Griffiths, a professor at Syracuse University who focuses on the dynamics of secession and the study of sovereignty. "In the long run, there will be another secessionist movement in the United States. It will just happen. No country is permanent. It will change. It will break apart in some way." One way of breaking apart requires mass death. The other requires political courage and the ability to face hard truths.

The first hard truth that needs facing is the most basic: that the United States no longer functions as a nation. The ideas that motivated its system no longer convince. The symbols that once unified its people no longer hold up. The country no longer makes sense.

The Appetite for Disunion

American tolerance for the idea of secession has been rapidly growing. In 2014, Reuters asked Americans, "Do you support or oppose the idea of your state peacefully withdrawing from the United States of America and the federal government?" One in four supported leaving. That's not one in four from states with active secessionist movements. That's one in four from the Union as a whole. America's taste for secessionism has never faded. Even in the country's most unified periods, it has always remained a sometimes violent force in the United States' history of overlapping and competing identities.

Since Trump's election, intellectuals on both sides have started arguing, tentatively, for an American separation. The *Federalist*, from the right, has argued that "we both now agree that living under the other side's value system is wholly unacceptable." The *New Republic*, from the left, shared the sentiment: "Let's face it, guys: We're done." American divorce, for the partisans, is a thought experiment, mostly just a chance to explain, in detail, how monstrous the other side is. "The GOP has many problems, but the Democratic Party has turned into something completely un-American. The United States was founded on two things: Judeo-Christian values and a limited federal government," the *Federalist* can say. The *New Republic* has a chance to indulge its contempt to the fullest: "Go ahead, keep on voting against your own economic interests to satisfy your need to control other people's bodies, sex lives, and recreational habits." More recent books, from both sides, have taken the issue much more seriously, such as *Break It Up* by Richard Kreitner and *Divided We Fall* by David French. Every year secession becomes more popular and every year its arguments become more legitimate.

The dream of disunion is far from a mere thought experiment at this point. Serious people, more of them all the time, are imagining realistic scenarios, planning, and organizing. As the identity of the United States dies, new identities and new loyalties—loyalties to countries that don't yet exist—are emerging.

Imagining Secession

The United States might well be better off as separate countries. How would it happen? For all the rhetoric of secession, for all the talk, almost no one, either in the media or in the political establishment, bothers with the specifics. They simply assume that if enough people support secession, it will happen. That assumption is naive. Secession is not easy. Ask any independence movement.

A national separation is a bureaucratic nightmare. Uncertainty over small questions of daily life like pensions and passports is a major reason why Scotland and Quebec are not independent nations today. How would the national debt be divided? Would dual citizenship be permitted? What amendments to the Constitution would be necessary to make secession possible? How would a state decide which country to belong to? What would the terms of new confederations look like? What would happen to the military?

If the pressure to split the United States grew, either through democratic means or through mass violence, how would the government of the United States respond? How would a new Philadelphia Convention, a de–Constitutional Convention, carve up the country? How would a broken America, with a half-legitimate president and fifty governors, work toward becoming future countries?

Where Would the Break Be?

The United States would have to agree to break up. It would have to know that the time had come. But then there is the question of how it would break. Along which lines? Who would break from whom? The first question facing the negotiators won't be "How should America be divided?" It will be "How is America divided?"

Simple political disagreement is not enough to make separation realistic. Regions don't tend to secede over political differences. "The main factor that drives the desire for independence, that makes it possible, is having a separate or ethnic identity," says Jason Sorens, a political scientist at Saint Anselm College in Manchester, New Hampshire, and a leading scholar of secessionist movements. "We don't have a state that has that identity." Puerto Rico isn't a state. Hawaii, the only non-white majority state, has an Indigenous population vastly outnumbered by Asian Americans.

That's not to say that political differences never lead to secessionist movements, but they are usually at least underpinned by regional identities. The Northern League of Italy is motivated by political differences between the northern states and the central government, but those states had also survived as independent states for centuries before Italian unification. Even in America's first civil war, the issue of slavery was, beyond question, the primary cause of the war, but secession was possible because the Southern partisans believed they were citizens of their states before they were citizens of their country. It is identity that matters, the sense of belonging to a nation. In Canada, Quebec shares, to a surprising degree, the same political vision as the rest of the country—on education, on health care, on the role of government—but Quebecois are a distinct people, defined by a language and a history. Therefore, they have a large and active separatist movement.

This is essential to understanding the possibility of American secession: mere political differences won't be enough. It is a question of identity and of whether the divisions of American politics are becoming identity differences. The anger overwhelming American politics, the hyper-partisanship, does not tend to separatism in itself. "You would need to see a gradual unmixing of these populations, and the cultivation of some idea of nation or consciousness. There are maybe glimmerings of that," Griffiths says. The dark glimmerings of the new separation are that, slowly but consistently, Americans are hiving themselves off into concentrated ethnic identities.

Difference as the Defining Feature of the United States

The beauty of the United States as a country is its mixtures. As a country, on all levels, it possesses an extraordinary ability to be many things at once. America is difference. Difference defines it. Differences of opinion. Differences of race. Differences of religion. Differences between the rich and the poor. America has always been overwhelmed with its multiplicity, a country that doesn't make a whole lot of sense by standards other than its own; it has always been a huge mass of contradictions. And any countries that could emerge out of the United States would themselves be masses of contradiction.

In 1981, *Washington Post* editor Joel Garreau had a bestseller with *The Nine Nations of North America*, in which he divided the continent into categories that included Ecotopia on the West Coast, New England on the East, and Dixie to the South. An updated 2011 version of Garreau's argument, *American Nations* by Colin Woodard, expanded the number to eleven. Regional identity is more complex than North and South. The South, for Woodard, contains six different nations. The East and the West Coasts contain multiple nations. And neither Garreau nor Woodard deal with Native Americans except as a lump. There are over five hundred federally registered tribes in the United States. And African Americans, as a distinct category, don't figure in either description.

The country is divided, not only by every available economic and social metric, but also by personality. In 2013, a group of British and American psychologists carved the United States into three "psychological regions" by large-scale psychometric analyses. "Psychological factors are likely to be the driving forces behind the individual-level behaviors that eventually get expressed in terms of macrolevel social and economic indicators," they hypothesized. They divided America into a "relaxed and creative region" on the West Coast "marked by low Extraversion and Agreeableness, very low Neuroticism, and very high Openness"; a "temperamental and uninhibited" region of the mid-Atlantic and Northeast "defined by low Extraversion, very low Agreeableness and Conscientiousness, very high Neuroticism, and moderately high Openness"; and the "friendly and conventional" region of the South and Middle, "defined by moderately high levels of Extraversion, Agreeableness, and Conscientiousness, moderately low Neuroticism, and very low Openness." Their research shows the emotional depth of the divide in the United States. "The most common explanations for the

American political divide point to religion, racial diversity, education or wealth," they write. "The present findings suggest another explanation for the differences, stemming from the psychological characteristics of residents."

The psychological characteristics play out in a variety of social and cultural differences, and those social and cultural differences can easily be defined geographically. Gun ownership is much more likely in the South and the Midwest than in the Northeast or the Pacific Coast. Proximity to abortion access is much more limited there. Corporal punishment in schools is still legal in much of the South and the Midwest. Church attendance is much higher. The percentages of marriages that are same-sex is much lower. And those important social differences—differences fundamentally in the way of life—correspond to which states voted Democratic and which states voted Republican in the 2016 election. And that political divide further corresponds to which states were free states and which states were slave states before the Civil War. These profound distinctions are geographical and they are entrenched. Blue America. Red America. They're real.

The Political Consequences of Division

The reason that Republicans and Democrats feel occupied is that both are. Blue America and Red America represent two identities, two styles of life, the mostly white and rural against the mostly multicultural and urban. In the 2018 election, density was the single strongest determinant of who voted Democratic and who voted Republican, with eight hundred people per square mile being the cutoff. Below that number, 66 percent vote Republican. Above it, 66 percent vote Democratic. The year 2018 saw the urban-rural divide in the United States become total: there are no urban Republican congressional districts left. The last one to fall was Staten Island. The pockets of political differences within states—Austin in Texas or the rural parts of southern Illinois—have come to resemble ethnic enclaves.

Each of these Americas promises a Utopia. Red America promises a country where government defers to individual rights, where the traditional family is the bedrock of society, where ordinary people live by the power of faith. Blue America promises a country of open ideas in which people can live by whatever values they choose and where distinct communities work together toward a more rational future. It's easy to flip these Utopias over. Red America is a bunch of macho hypocrite rednecks. Blue America is a bunch of latte-sipping wimps. Each side accuses the other of hating America, which is only another way of saying that both hate what the other means by America. The pleasure of contempt for the other side has launched media empires: Rush Limbaugh and Fox News for the red, Jon Stewart and MSNBC for the blue. Loathing is the principal emotion that America's political entertainment industry sells.

On both sides, the sense of being under occupation dominates. It doesn't matter where you go or who you talk to. The Black teenagers in Baltimore and St. Louis feel under occupation by the police. The ranchers in Texas and Oregon feel under occupation by the federal government. Every political faction operates under a siege mentality—the Democrats from the Republican political machine; the Republicans from demographics, from immigration, from popular culture. Everyone wants to build a wall of one kind or another.

The geographical divide between the competing American Utopias means that, in every election, whoever loses comes to feel like they've been dominated by a foreign power. The response is always the same: Begin by delegitimizing the president—"Obama is a Kenyan" or "Trump is not my president"—then proceed by arguing for a shift in power away from the federal government. Red America has argued for states' rights from well before the Civil War. Blue America is finally starting to come around. "If I live in a blue city, I have my way of life. If you live in a red state or a red city, you have your way of life," the urbanist Richard Florida argued in a recent interview. "The way to lower the stakes is to make the Imperial presidency and the nation-state less important." The way across the political divide, in other words, is to accept it. Federalism is tolerable only when my side is in power. The appetite for secession is always highest in presidential out-party states.

And if you imagine a miraculous political figure emerging from the American middle to fulfill the by now cliché political imperative to "unite, not divide," the bad news is your dreams have already come true. There was a president who preached unity and hope. The other side insisted he was a Kenyan and brought a man who denied his citizenship to power. Significant portions of the United States believed that their government was controlled by a foreign power, as a significant number of Americans came to believe that Russian interference was the primary explanation for the election of Donald Trump. Biden in power has changed nothing. He is most effective insofar as he has abandoned bipartisanship rather than restored it.

The Big Sort Reconsidered

America is already countries within the same country. In 2004, the journalist Bill Bishop coined the term the "big sort" to describe how Americans of different political beliefs are self-selecting away from each other. The choices people make aren't necessarily political: few people move from, say, Los Angeles to rural Texas explicitly because they want to be around Republicans rather than Democrats. But as partisan politics comes to define Americans' sense of themselves, the decisions they make about who they are and what kind of lives they want to lead inevitably place them in one tribe or another. They want to be in Texas rather than California, and that means the people they want to be around tend to be Republicans rather than Democrats. People who move to Texas go there for its spirit of freedom and individualism as well as its opportunities; they just happen to move into Republican territory.

Since 2004, the big sort has increased in intensity, both nationally and within states. And the trend is pretty much exactly what you'd expect. It's bicoastal, with more Democrats moving to New England and to the mid-Atlantic and Pacific regions and more Republicans moving to the Midwest and the South. This is the key to the future of the United States as a political entity. The polarization is geographical. Americans with different politics are moving farther away from each other physically as well as ideologically. The separation feeds back into the political system. More states become single-party states, like California and Texas. Ideological unity replaces open debates. The geography of the national government, and the way it apportions power, become distorted. Huge geographical inequalities are baked into the system of government—which is, after all, nearly 250 years old. Sixty-two senators represent one quarter of the American population. Six senators represent another quarter. The same discrepancy, though to a much lesser extent, causes presidential victories without the popular vote, which further skews the power imbalance.

Within that big sort, there's also been a small sort. American politicians have spent decades breaking their country up into ever more bizarrely contorted districts in order to engineer victories. The technological sophistication of gerrymandering, the quantity and quality of information available for carving up regions into noncompetitive strongholds, keeps advancing. The name of the game is "incumbent protection," and it works. Whoever is in power, on either side, forges the structures to keep themselves in power. Everybody wants democracy but nobody wants democracy. Gerrymandering leads, quite naturally, to voter suppression, which is increasingly an overt tactic. Once you've started making your opponents' votes matter less by fixing the district, why not make it harder for your opponents to vote in the first place by moving the polling places to less convenient locations? Once you've done that, why not simply suppress their vote by any means available?

Each small decision, undertaken for tactical reasons, erodes, slowly but surely, the political system as a whole. The American people don't want to be around the other side and whenever possible choose not to be. Their leaders don't want to engage in meaningful competition of political ideas and don't need to. America is being shaken like a sieve, separating Democrat from Republican into political, social, intellectual, geographical fortresses. The sorting makes life easier for everybody. The only thing that suffers is American democracy.

The Status of Secessionist Movements in the United States

The men who are planning the destruction of the United States are cheerful men, open, frank, and ambitious. They are very American in their plots against America.

Daniel Miller, head of the Texas Nationalist Movement, lives in Nederland, a town of 17,000 on the Gulf Coast. The TNM is the latest iteration of a decades-old movement. Like the Scottish National Party or many other separatist movements, it began in lunatic fringes and fractured sects divided by method and ideology and then coalesced. The Republic of Texas movement in the 1970s, by Miller's description, "splintered into a thousand pieces" after two years. In the 1990s, five Texas separatists were involved in a standoff with federal authorities. Some were shot. The others were sentenced to extensive prison sentences. "When we were founded in 2005, any of the polling data we could find put us in single digits. And it hovered that way for a long time," Miller says. Fast-forward to 2014, around the time of the Scottish Independence referendum, when Reuters/Ipsos polled Texans and found that 36 percent believed that Texas should secede. And that was during a period of relative political unity in hindsight.

The California separatist movement is much newer and so less established. But in January 2017, Reuters revealed that 32 percent of Californians supported California becoming its own independent state, a number roughly in line with several other polls at the time. Another 13 percent weren't sure. The leader of the Calexit movement, Marcus Ruiz Evans, lives in Fresno, a city of half a million in the San Joaquin Valley. The election of Trump spiked interest in the movement, but, for Evans at least, the desire to escape American politics dated to the Iraq War, widely supported in the United States as a whole but not by California. Diverging politics has led to profound contempt for the federal government, which Evans calls "a horrible abusive relationship that's gone on for thirty years."

Unlike separatist movements in the rest of the world, neither the Texas Nationalist Movement nor the Calexit movement have formed their own parties. They don't need to. California and Texas are single-party states. Democrats have not won a statewide election in Texas since 1994. The Republicans have taken Texas in every presidential election since 1976. They have controlled the state legislature since 2003. In California, only 25 percent of registered voters are Republicans. San Francisco has not had a Republican mayor since 1964. Democrats in California hold every statewide office. Because of their unusual ballot system, where the top two candidates face each other in Senate races, Democrats run against Democrats. America may be Democratic and Republican, but Texas and California are not. Both states have, in a sense, already separated from half the country.

Because both states are single-party states, Calexit and Texit advocates press their cases through the dominant party, whose partisan identity is already built on the rejection of the other side. At the Texas GOP convention in 2016, the Texas secessionists came two votes shy of having the matter reach the convention floor for a full vote. The number of GOP county conventions that passed independence resolutions remains in dispute, but it's somewhere between 10 and 22 out of 270, which is more than the single county that passed such a resolution in 2012.

"We have got support of rank-and-file Republican voters," Miller explains. "The challenge that we have run into is that when it comes to leadership in Texas, particularly the Republican leadership, they all have their eyes set on a federal office, and the paycheck and benefits that comes with it." Republican leaders in Texas play a dangerous game. They flirt with separatism but won't go all the way. They know the majority of their base loves the rhetoric of Texas independence but they also know it's Utopian. Miller blames careerism more than cynicism. "The leadership talks out of both

sides of their mouth. They love to tease supporters of independence
to get their votes. They one hundred percent every time fail to
deliver." Former governor Rick Perry often mused about the possibilities of secession, but it never amounted to anything.

Miller recalls meeting with Rick Perry's legislative director, a
former state senator, who promised that Perry would never run
for federal office, and within two weeks he had announced his
candidacy. "You'll hear them read these applause lines. The current governor, Greg Abbott, is the absolute worst at this," Miller
says. "He loves, when he gives his stump speeches, to the throw
the line out there, 'If Texas were its own nation,' then he rattles
off some wonderful economic statistic about how we measure up
against all the nations of the world. Invariably it's his largest applause line. It gives people this mistaken impression that Abbott is
really a fan, maybe secretly, of Texas independence. But Abbott is
one of the guys who works overtime behind the scenes to torpedo
a lot of things we have done." The politicians like Abbott who indulge in separatist rhetoric know they won't be tested, so they can
play games. When Scots or Catalans or Quebecois say they want to
split, they mean it. Abbott is indulging in dreams. The rhetoric is
allowed to expand, to float free of consequence, at least for him, at
least for the moment.

Californian politicians indulge in separatist rhetoric less often
than Texans do, although it is sometimes blurted out. Jerry Brown,
on a visit to China, spoke of his state like it was its own country.
"It is a little bold to talk about California-China partnership as if
we were a separate nation, but we are a separate nation," he said.
"We're a state of mind." Even if he was joking, California under
his leadership has resisted the federal government with far more
than just talk. They have veered toward nullification. Sometimes

they have more than veered. Attorney General Jeff Sessions came to California to speak against their policy of sanctuary cities because it was in violation of federal authority. "There is no secession," the attorney general felt required to insist. "Federal law is the supreme law of the land. I would invite any doubters to go to Gettysburg, or to the tombstones of John C. Calhoun and Abraham Lincoln. This matter has been settled." Well, has it? That's the question. Maybe the matter was once settled. It is becoming unsettled again.

The Constitutionality of Secession

Secession is unconstitutional—that part is settled. You will not find a single serious constitutional scholar who believes that secession, under any condition, is legal. Both the Texas and California separatists have their arguments about why separation is constitutional, drawn from esoteric readings of *Texas v. White*, an 1869 decision about the legality of state bonds, but generally the consensus is bipartisan on the point. "I cannot imagine that such a question could ever reach the Supreme Court," Antonin Scalia wrote in 2006. "To begin with, the answer is clear. If there was any constitutional issue resolved by the Civil War, it is that there is no right to secede." The separatists respond with the obvious fact Scalia admits: technically, the constitutionality of secession has never been tested in the Supreme Court.

It is true that the court system has never had to deal with the constitutionality of secession, but that's mainly because the first section of the Fourteenth Amendment reads: "All persons born or naturalized in the United States, and subject to the jurisdiction thereof, are citizens of the United States and of the State wherein they reside. No State shall make or enforce any law which shall abridge the privileges or immunities of citizens of the United States; nor shall any State deprive any person of life, liberty, or property, without due process of law; nor deny to any person within its jurisdiction the equal protection of the laws." You're an American first. Then you're a citizen of a state. The state cannot make laws that deny citizens their rights as Americans. If Texas were to secede, they could not deny any Texan their American citizenship. Their laws would be subject to American laws. Therefore, Texas cannot constitutionally secede.

The text of the law doesn't really matter, though. Some questions are bigger than law. David A. Strauss, a leading scholar of the Constitution, wrote in 1998: "Before the Civil War, there was a lively and inconclusive debate over whether the Constitution permitted states to secede. There is no longer any such debate; the issue was settled by the Civil War. No one today would seriously advance the position that the Constitution permits secession, at least the kind that the Confederacy attempted. Where is the text that settled this question? The answer, of course, is that this question, like other important constitutional questions, is decided by something other than the text." That's what Scalia was saying, too. The text of the law was determined by historical events, not the other way around. There once was one hell of an argument about whether secession was legal. It happened in the 1860s. About 600,000 Americans died in that argument.

Only a few countries possess legal machinery for secession anyway. Canada has made arrangements for what the acceptable conditions would be for Quebec to separate. Britain has done the same in the case of Scotland. But in most countries in the world, secession is illegal, just as it is in the United States. That's not to say it doesn't happen. The laws adapt to the reality of history.

Meanwhile, secessionism grows. "It's not grandpa that places the Lone Star over the Stars and Stripes, but his grandchildren," Miller reports. In Texas, the movement is growing fastest among Democrats and African Americans.

What the Negotiations Would Look Like

The negotiations would be like a divorce. The lawyers would pick over the bones. In offices on neutral territory, the heat of passionate loathing would worm its way into the coldness of bureaucratic reasoning.

We know a great deal about what such a divorce between regions would look like, because they're happening all the time. "If you want to become a recognized independent state, that means you become a recognized member of the United Nations," Griffiths says. "There's a club of states. To get into the club, you would put in an application. If an application comes to them, they put it in a little group from the office of legal affairs." If the working group thinks the application is too trivial, they reject it. If they think it's serious enough, which they do by asking other states, then it goes to the Security Council. "The Security Council decides on whether or not to support the application. It has to win by a three-fifths vote without any vetoes. That's key. If that works, it goes to the General Council, which generally rubber-stamps the Security Council's decision." So what that means is that the Security Council is the arbiter, but the Security Council almost always agrees when the application has proceeded that far. The Kurds have never applied for independence to the Security Council because they know they'll lose. "A tremendous amount of weight is given to the home state from which you want to secede," Griffiths says. It's "the home state veto." So the United States, if it wanted to, could easily hold up any state asking for sovereignty. It would have the Security Council seat, and it would have the home state veto.

"Let's imagine that the Texas Nationalist Movement really made some headway," Griffiths proposes. They call a referendum, and there's a groundswell, and it looks like they have a majority of Texans on board. "The United States will work hard to defeat it on the grounds that it's illegal." But it wouldn't matter. "Most countries in the world, at some level, to varying degrees of strength, declare that secession is illegal. That doesn't mean those things become obstacles down the line." Politics comes before the law when borders are in question. "Secession is more of a political conflict than a legal one." If huge majorities declare they want Texas to separate, the legalities will become irrelevant. If it gets to 70 percent, "then the United States is going to have a real problem."

The negotiators would be faced with a pair of dilemmas. The first would be from the point of view of the US government. "A big difference between Scotland and Quebec and Texas is the way that Texas is defined administratively," Griffiths says. A Texas separation would be a precedent-setting problem. "If the government doesn't show its commitment to stopping the Texas Independence movement, it gives pathways to other states to independence." Scotland and Quebec are already distinct political entities. Not US states. "Jurisdictionally, they're all the same," Griffiths says. If one state leaves, where does it end?

There would be a dilemma on Texas's side, too. They would have a moral right to secede, and they would sense massive pressure from their supporters to declare independence. But such romantic ideas of statehood, derived from the eighteenth and nineteenth centuries, would have little purchase in the twenty-first century. It's all very well to imagine a bunch of independence-minded Texans raising their rifles in the air and shouting, "Don't mess with Texas!" and defying the world in the name of their freedom. That's all well and good until nobody will land an airplane in a Texas airport. And a separate Texas wouldn't have the power of the current United States in global negotiations. They would just be another midsize country with no history and no connections.

"There's only one sovereignty game," as Griffiths says. Everybody needs to get into the same club, and that club is the UN, which would require US approval. Some states separate without UN recognition. It does happen. Kosovo is not a recognized state. "To get plugged into the global economy, you need to be a UN member," Griffiths points out. "You have states out there that are quasi-states: Somaliland, Nagorno-Karabakh, Northern Cyprus; they sort of endure as states. But it's difficult. They're sort of handicapped. They can't do international exchange with foreign banks. They can't have an international post address. So they're forced to use the black market. All of these things are denied them because they're not a sovereign state." If you want to go to Northern Cyprus, you have to fly to Turkey, because it's the only country that recognizes Northern Cyprus. So the planes touch down for a minute in Istanbul and then reroute to Ercan.

Both sides would have a lot to lose and little to gain by separation. As in the aftermath of the collapse of the Soviet Union, the international community's first priority would be to denuclearize Texas or any new state formed out of American collapse. The second priority would be to prevent bloodshed. And, needless to say, Texas or any other remnants of the United States would no longer qualify as a superpower.

The fact that there is no established legal mechanism for separation in the United States—that there is in fact a massive counter-mechanism in the Constitution—is paradoxically what makes the idea of separation so dangerous. If the right to secession was determined by facts outside the text, then facts outside the text can determine it again. "If the Civil War did settle this issue, then no one would even be discussing it," Miller says, which is his most convincing argument. If Texas or California declared themselves independent, would the federal government bring them back by force? Could they bring them back by force when 48 percent of American soldiers believe it's a state's right to leave? Secession may be unconstitutional, but it sure is American. What could be more American than the idea that "in the Course of human events it becomes necessary for one people to dissolve the political bands which have connected them with another"? America is founded on the right to break up political unities.

That's what makes America separatism so fascinating, so distinct. The separatists love America even in their hatred. Both Texas and California separatists are obsessed with proving that their desire to separate is constitutional. It's genuinely weird. Everywhere else in the world, unconstitutionality is a moot point. Quebec separatists do not worry about whether their departure would violate the spirit or letter of the British North America Act. The Catalans have no interest in proving they are maintaining the foundational Spanish political order. But Texan and Californian separatists do. "We're not withdrawing from America," Miller says. "We're withdrawing from an economic and political union called the United States of America. And the two are not the same." They are living their original national contradiction to the full—patriotic treason and treasonous patriotism.

These are movements grounded in a sense of loss. Separatists in America love America, and their love has emerged in the most twisted possible form: They have devoted themselves to the basic proposition that America is no longer possible in the United States of America.

Do the Separatists Mean It?

These weird American separatists and their tortured adoration and contempt for their country are not new. The United States has always provoked a unique mixture of love and hatred among its most passionate patriots. "The Man Without a Country," a short story by Edward Everett Hale, was a classic in its time, taught in high schools all over America; it produced that semi-religious devotion that high school literature sometimes elicits. During the bicentennial, there was even a gravestone set up in front of the Covington County Courthouse in Andalusia, Alabama, dedicated to the memory of Philip Nolan, the fictional character at the heart of the story.

The *Atlantic* published the story in December 1863, right in the teeth of the Civil War. "The Man Without a Country" was written at a time when America was unsure if it was a country and about another time when America was unsure if it was a country. Aaron Burr, vice president under Thomas Jefferson and the man who killed Alexander Hamilton in a duel, was charged with treason in 1807. It was alleged that he planned to establish a separate country in the Southwest. Burr was eventually acquitted. But Philip Nolan, the fictional coconspirator with Burr in "The Man Without a Country," was not. At his trial, in a fit of rage, he shouts out "D—n the United States! I wish I may never hear of the United States again!" His punishment is the fulfillment of his wish: "Prisoner, hear the sentence of the Court! The Court decides, subject to the approval of the President, that you never hear the name of the United States again." They even take away his naval buttons, which bear the inscription "US."

Not only are Nolan's fellow sailors forbidden from mentioning their home country; they have to cut any reference to it out of his books. "Right in the midst of one of Napoleon's battles, or one of Canning's speeches, poor Nolan would find a great hole, because on the back of the page of that paper there had been an advertisement of a packet for New York, or a scrap from the President's message."

He craves facts about American politics above all. Sex is as nothing to his desire to know about his homeland. At one point in the story, because the other sailors need his stateroom, he's invited to a ball on the ship. Nolan meets a woman he knew from home and tries to squeeze some information out of her:

"And what do you hear from home, Mrs. Graff?"

And that splendid creature looked through him. Jove! how she must have looked through him!

"Home!! Mr. Nolan!!! I thought you were the man who never wanted to hear of home again!"—and she walked directly up the deck to her husband, and left poor Nolan alone, as he always was.—He did not dance again.

Meanwhile, the country keeps changing and Nolan has no idea. He belongs to what he doesn't understand. And he loves what he no longer belongs to. His ship, on its endless sea journey, encounters a slave ship. The captain of Nolan's vessel thinks only of returning the slaves back to their homelands. Nolan finds their longing for home unbearably moving, and he gives a speech to one of the youngsters on board:

> ". . . Remember, boy, that behind all these men you have to do with, behind officers, and government, and people even, there is the Country Herself, your Country, and that you belong to Her as you belong to your own mother. Stand by Her, boy, as you would stand by your mother, if those devils there had got hold of her to-day!"

"The Man Without a Country" is in one sense a very simple story, one that you could happily read to boys that you're about to send off to war, a strange but palatable fable of patriotism. But there is also a paradox knotted in its center: Every patriot hates his or her country. When you love your country, that's when it drives you crazy. You can only love your country when you imagine it rather than live in it. You can only love home from the boat.

At the end of "The Man Without a Country," Philip Nolan is lying in bed; his room has become a shrine to the country he cursed.

> The stars and stripes were triced up above and around a picture of Washington, and he had painted a majestic eagle, with lightnings blazing from his beak and his foot just clasping the whole globe, which his wings overshadowed. The dear old boy saw my glance, and said, with a sad smile, 'Here, you see, I have a country!' And then he pointed to the foot of his bed, where I had not seen before a great map of the United States, as he had drawn it from memory, and which he had there to look upon as he lay. Quaint, queer old

names were on it, in large letters: 'Indiana Territory,' 'Mississippi Territory,' and 'Louisiana Territory,' as I suppose our fathers learned such things . . .

As Nolan lies dying, a friend named Danforth finally tells him all that has happened to America—of the states that have joined the Union, the triumphs of the young country. But he can't bring himself to talk about the Civil War, which was underway during the story's composition. Even in the end, even by a compassionate friend, Nolan has to be deceived about the nature of his country.

"The Man Without a Country" is a profound, dark little story about what it means to belong. Is a country a collection of vaguely like-minded individuals participating, by choice or by the accident of birth, in a collective project? Or is it closer to a family with arrangements, with stories and symbols and rituals, that keep it splitting into factions? For Philip Nolan, dying aboard his ship, the country he loved was a half-remembered dream. And that's the point: the more distant the memory, the more vague the dream, the more possible it is to love your country.

Dan Miller and Marcus Ruiz Evans are motivated by love of countries that are half-imagined dreams, half-remembered fantasies. Countries without the embarrassment of existence are the easiest to love. For Evans, California is the only place in the United States where he belongs, where there is "an acceptance of a range of different diversities, culturally and ideologically. This is the place where you can come and be accepted." Miller's love of Texas is more forthright, though more ethereal. "It's this intangible quality. It's hard to put words on it. I love Texas because I'm a Texan. My first ancestor fought with Sam Houston at the battle of San Jacinto. There is this mindset, this allure. There is just something about the people, about the land, about the climate, about the history. There is something about all of it. At the end of the day, it's just my home. It's home." It is no surprise that it is so easy to convince people of the value of secession. Our homes are easy to love. The government, which becomes visible most commonly in failure, is easy to hate.

And when your country is a dream, how can any reality be more than a disappointment?

Overcoming America

The Texas and California separatist movements are only the two largest. There are dozens of others. But separatist movements are marginal forces for disunion. The rising number of Americans who are disillusioned with their country is a more central threat: they don't want America's differences. They can no longer tolerate America's contradictions.

Richard Spencer is the most prominent figure in the alt-right movement, and there has been a push, in the progressive press, against describing him in any other terms but monstrosity. There is certainly enough monstrosity in Richard Spencer. He has described his opponents as "fucking kikes" and "fucking octoroons." "Those pieces of fucking shit get ruled by people like me," he said in an audiotape taken clandestinely at the Charlottesville rally. But if you only acknowledge Spencer's monstrosity, you will never understand the significance of his threat. He is not some prison house Nazi with "Born to Lose" tattooed on his neck. The man is charming. The charm is the threat.

He is educated and he has plans to build a national white identity and out of that identity a state. When you ask Spencer how he would envision his ethnonationalist state, he blithely mentions the Japanese constitution and Israel's "Law of Return." The new racism is not atavistic. It is not reactionary or stupid. Spencer believes, for instance, in reparations to African Americans: "White people have committed historical crimes against Africans, and those crimes have been detrimental to both peoples." He just wants to pay reparations to people who live in another country, not his.

Spencer is a white nationalist, not an American nationalist—a key distinction. "I am profoundly ambivalent about the American project," he tells me. The identity in his identity politics is not American. The United States, after all, is African in part. American culture, in almost all of its distinctive forms, is a mixture of European and African diasporas. Demographic change is the source of the turmoil. But demographic change is not something that is happening in America or happening to America. Demographic change *is* America, and Spencer knows it. "White people have assumed that they are America, and it's dawning on them that they aren't." He has another, more ominous way of putting it: "I think we need to overcome America."

Spencer's whiteness is fragile; it senses itself under threat. That sense of white fragility is not new but it is quickly coalescing. To any sensible person, looking at America's history on voting rights and real estate and incarceration, white supremacy looks like the prime motivation of the history of the country: an elaborate scheme to deny African Americans the status of free property-holding voters. But white supremacy is always experienced as supremacy about to be lost. It has possessed an imminent sense of erasure from its beginning. The original feature film *The Birth of a Nation* (1915) was an epic of white people under threat from a multicultural political elite. Obama quoted Faulkner in his great 2008 speech

on race—"The past isn't dead. It's not even past"—but Faulkner
was lamenting his own family's losses, not the crimes of his people
against African Americans. Whiteness is inherently nostalgic. In
The Great Gatsby, Nick Carraway encounters a vision as he crosses
Blackwell's Island into Manhattan, a vision of hypermodernity:
"A limousine passed us, driven by a white chauffeur, in which sat
three modish negroes, two bucks and a girl. I laughed aloud as the
yolks of their eyeballs rolled toward us in haughty rivalry." That's
the future Carraway sees, crossing into the city. White Americans
have always suspected that America is not essentially a white country and that their whiteness is incompatible with its future.

At one point as we chat, I ask Spencer how he feels at Trump
rallies, whose spectators share none of his calm, reasoned articu-
lateness. He must have more in common with any African American graduate student, I suggest. He attended the University of
Chicago.

Even the idea that he would share more with a Black person
than with a white person makes him squirm.

"They're still my people," he says about Trump's crowds.
"They're still people that I have much, much more in common
with than any African American."

Underneath the impeccable manners, under the charm, lies a
profound contempt for Blackness itself, which all the manners do
nothing to alleviate.

"Most people do want to be around their own kind. It's hard to
explain because it's so deeply ingrained. You care about your own
family more than you care about other people's."

And so there it comes down to the real question: Who is the
American family? The old, old question.

"The only thing that is different now is that these conversations are happening in public," DeRay Mckesson tells me. Mckesson is the most prominent leader of Black Lives Matter, arrested in Baton Rouge for protesting, a major force behind Campaign Zero, a plan for the comprehensive police reform that would provide a real policy solution to the crisis between African Americans and the police.

"Trump isn't the first person to say 'build a wall,'" Mckesson says. "Trump made popular birtherism, but he wasn't the first person to say it."

The process that Black Lives Matter confronts runs deeper.

"The Civil Rights Act still emerged in a context of people pushing back. People got teargassed and water hosed. That was the status quo pushing back. And people still overcame."

There was that word again: "overcoming." Richard Spencer and DeRay Mckesson are not comparable human beings. One belongs to a movement based on the fundamental stupidity of racial pride and celebrates genocide. The other is looking for social justice and equality under the law. But, between them, you can see the cleaving, the unsettling, of the United States. They both want to overcome America in all its glorious, ludicrous contradiction.

The hyper-partisanship that is dominating American politics is, at least in part, the emergence of ethnic identity. The Republican Party has become a white rump party. The difference between the Democratic Party and the Republican Party over the past thirty years is that Republicanism became the party of white resentment of growing diversity, while the Democratic Party became the party of imposed multiculturalism. The racial resentment levels have nothing to do with age, so do not expect hope from that quarter. The reason young Americans poll as less racist is only because they are more diverse. In 2019, two researchers who study racial affect undertook a "cross-generational analysis of the nature and role of racial attitudes in the 21st century." They found "younger Whites are not bringing about any meaningful change in the aggregate levels of racial resentment." And as we saw in Dispatch Two, as diversity increases, it only increases the sense of white threat.

For 240 years, America was a white settler country that could pretend it contained transcendent post-ethnic values. That pretense survives, at the moment, in a kind of inertia. For how long? "We could imagine that changing over a couple of generations. We could imagine political divisions growing deep enough in the United States that some states rely on those political divisions to see themselves as a distinct nation," Jason Sorens says. "There is something that could lead to the formation of a separate nation."

Separate ethnic identities are emerging: America as a white settler republic, America as a multicultural democracy. You can have one or the other. Both cannot survive except as distinct countries.

The Iconoclasm

Remember: countries don't tend to separate because of political division. Countries separate because of the emergence of national consciousness with territorial divisions, "concentrated ethnonationalist groups," according to Ryan Griffiths. Have the divisions within the United States grown to the point at which they constitute divided identities? The mechanism of identity is symbolism. And the symbols that once unified the States are crumbling everywhere. America is in the middle of a grand iconoclasm. In other countries and at other times, the breaking up of images has frequently been a prelude to civil war.

An Example of American Iconoclasm: Silent Sam

On August 20, 2018, at the University of North Carolina at Chapel Hill, the youth of America hacked the Confederate statue known as Silent Sam from his foundation, tossed him over in a gleeful moan of collective ecstasy, stomped him from his safety and permanence and solidity. A few in the crowd began, as if in some ancient ritual they were just inventing, to cover his face with crumbly mud they had scraped with their bare hands from the soggy earth.

"It was honestly the best moment I've ever had," Maya Little says, remembering the downfall. She's a graduate student in history, an organizer, the woman who threw her own blood mixed with red paint on the statue at an event a few months before Silent Sam fell. "It made a great creaking sound, and everyone got quiet. A second later, everyone started hugging and cheering. Then it started raining. It was just a really beautiful moment." Jake Sullivan, a UNC alumnus, witnessed the fall, too. "I was just deeply sad," he remembers. "Sure we get angry before or after, but when I see the face of that brave young man buried in the mud and dirt he figuratively fought and died for and privileged white kids awkwardly kick and spit on him, there's nothing else for someone like me to be but deeply, deeply sad. How did we get here? How is this okay? Who are these people?" Maya Little is African American and Jake Sullivan is the North Carolina division chief for the Sons of Confederate Veterans. The United States is a country of Maya Littles and Jake Sullivans. They possess different meanings. They have different histories, belong to different peoples. They already belong, in a sense, to different countries, except that they happen to live in the same country. All they share is a spirit of fury.

Even ten years ago, the UNC administration would have

known just what to do after the desecration of a statue: repair the damage and move on. After the assassination of Martin Luther King Jr. in 1968, a hammer and sickle in bright red, yellow, and green paint covered the statue; the next morning it was scrubbed clean. Even in 2015, the administration removed a "Black Lives Matter" tag when it was sprayed there during a protest. But cleaning is different from restoring. It's one thing to want a Confederate monument on your campus to be clean. It's quite another to raise one back up.

Maya Little remembers her first glimpse of Silent Sam as she crossed the UNC campus in the summer of 2016. "You see it immediately when you go to McCorkle Place, which is the forefront of campus. It's this beautiful quad with all these beautiful buildings that frame it. All these buildings were built by slaves." Sam's original location is very much an element of his symbolic power. "He stands at the front of campus, facing north, and not just the North that the South fought against but also against the north part of Chapel Hill, which is a historically Black part of town," Little explains. "So, imagine anyone from that neighborhood walking towards UNC: What is the first thing they see when they walk onto campus? It's an armed Confederate soldier." To put Silent Sam back where he was would be to put his meanings back in their original place.

That's just what Jake Sullivan wants. He is fighting for restoration in many senses. In November of 2018, he began organizing a protest flyover, and within days the state membership of the Sons of Confederate Veterans raised the money. Originally, they planned to fly on November 3, the date of the UNC homecoming game, but a malfunction in the twin-engine plane prevented takeoff. Their next opportunity was Veterans Day, which suited their purposes fine. "Confederate veterans are American veterans in every sense of the word," Sullivan says. This time the weather was clear and calm, and the plane worked. A banner with the Confederate flag and the message RESTORE SILENT SAM NOW flew over Chapel Hill, Durham, and Raleigh.

The law is entirely on the side of Sullivan and the Sons of Confederate Veterans. So are most North Carolinians, 53.7 percent of whom support the restoration, a number that rises to 66.8 percent of white voters. In 2015, in direct response to protests over Silent Sam, the North Carolina Senate unanimously passed a ban on the removal of Confederate monuments. "An object of remembrance may not be relocated to a museum, cemetery, or mausoleum unless it was originally placed at such a location." There is a solution to the problem of Silent Sam. It's not that hard to figure out. Other jurisdictions have moved Confederate monuments to museums or cemeteries, positions of respect that are not offensively prominent. That way, the Sons of Confederate Veterans can honor their ancestors, and African Americans don't have to confront monuments to white supremacy as they walk the streets. North Carolina's state legislature has made that obvious and easy solution impossible. "An object of remembrance located on public property may not be permanently removed and may only be relocated," the law decreed.

The administrators are trapped. If they put Silent Sam back, they're asking for riots. And you can debate what "jurisdiction" means, and you can debate what "similar prominence" means, and you can debate whether the state law is in violation of Title VI and Title IX, but "may not be relocated to a museum" is surely clear enough. They cannot ship the thing elsewhere. The activists on both sides, highly organized and entirely capable of violence, would refuse compromise anyway. "If UNC officials have already said countless times that the memorial is at the 'gateway' of the University, how can there be any other place of similar prominence on campus?" Sullivan points out, and he's not wrong. Maya Little has a simpler proposal for what to do with the statue: "They should leave the monument in the ground, in the dirt where it fell, and put a plaque up commemorating the people who have fought against it." That will be tough on the alumni tour.

As the old myths fall, the myths of the first Civil War are falling first. The war's memory weighs so much more heavily in the South than the North because the devastation was so much more extreme there. South Carolina lost 60 percent of its landed value, and 20,000 of its 60,000 white men of military age over the course of the war. All that suffering, all that death, must have had some noble purpose, right? The South's myth of the "lost cause" relied on "states' rights" for justification. The North, for its part, developed the myth that they had fought the war to end slavery. Both are only dubiously reflected in the historical record. On Lincoln's memorial, a quote from his second inaugural loads the mass death of the war he prosecuted with the significance of a redemptive divine retribution for the crime of slavery: "He gives to both North and South this terrible war as the woe due to those by whom the offense came." But even after the war's outbreak, Lincoln was clear enough about his motivations. "My paramount object in this struggle is to save the Union and is not either to save or to destroy slavery," he wrote in a letter. "If I could save the Union without freeing any slave I would do it." The value of Black lives was always incidental.

Christy Coleman, the former CEO of the American Civil War Museum in Richmond, is wrestling with America's competing mythologies at the exact moment when the old symbols and the old stories have stopped working. She began her career in museum work by attending Civil War reenactments and playing a slave—a gutsy business, inserting the story of human property into historical memory that wanted to forget that part of the story. She knows why the lost cause remains such a powerful force in Southern life. "When you're talking about that level of trauma, particularly to the white South, there is this need to reconcile their grief," she says. "And the way they did that was to take slavery out of the picture." The essence of the lost-cause ideology is a forgetting within remembering, an amnesia necessary to have a morally coherent history.

Northern triumph required its own form of forgetting within memory. "When the North and the South do reconcile, one thing they reconcile over pretty easily is white supremacy. That's the first thing," Coleman says. Union and Confederate soldiers gathered together to cement their brotherhood in arms in ceremonies that raised the monuments to the Confederate dead—monuments like Silent Sam. Southern fiction imagined an antebellum South of "happy darkies" retelling romances between Union soldiers and Southern belles—wildly popular in the North as well as the South. Black veterans—there were more than 200,000—were disinvited to the celebrations. You might say that the North won the war and the South won the peace. But that's not entirely accurate. The North won progress. The South won heritage. The North won the future. The South won the past. And it is not clear at all which is more powerful. The reconciliation is "how we chose to lie to each other for a hundred and fifty years," as Coleman puts it.

The irony of figures like Silent Sam is that, far from representing the overcoming of America's internal hostilities, they represent their resumption by other means. Union brigadier general James S. Brisbin was sent to pacify the white South during Reconstruction. "These people are not loyal; they are only conquered," he wrote back. "I tell you there is not as much loyalty in the South today as there was the day Lee surrendered to Grant. The moment they lost their cause in the field they set about to gain by politics what they had failed to obtain by force of arms." In the disputes over the election of Rutherford Hayes in 1876, the election with the highest turnout in American history (over 80 percent), both sides claimed victories in Florida, Louisiana, and South Carolina. An informal deal was struck to give Hayes the presidency in exchange for pulling federal troops from the South, essentially ceding the whole region to white supremacy. The Redeemers came back to power and immediately disenfranchised Black voters. They called it the Compromise of 1877. Compromise was the cost of the union.

Silent Sam itself was another such compromise. At 4:30 p.m. on the afternoon of June 2, 1913, Julian Carr, an industrialist and supporter of the Ku Klux Klan who received an honorary degree from UNC, inaugurated the statue with a speech in which he bragged about his courage in flogging an African American woman: "One hundred yards from where we stand, less than ninety days perhaps after my return from Appomattox, I horse-whipped a negro wench until her skirts hung in shreds, because upon the streets of this quiet village she had publicly insulted and maligned a Southern lady, and then rushed for protection to these University buildings where was stationed a garrison of a hundred Federal soldiers. I performed the pleasing duty in the immediate presence of the entire garrison, and for thirty nights afterwards slept with a double-barrel shot gun under my head." The record does not relate whether the audience chuckled at this anecdote, but after the Carr speech, they marched to the monument itself for the unveiling, and sang "Tenting on the Old Camp Ground," an old, mournful tune of soldiers who just want to be home. Even at the inauguration of the statue, it told a double story: the story of white supremacy and the story of the sufferings of ordinary men.

The great-great-grandson of Jefferson Davis, the president of the Confederacy, has devoted a fair portion of his life to trying to fathom the crossroads where those stories meet. "If we forget the evil that has created our history, we're doomed to repeat it," Bertram Hayes-Davis says. "Those folks that want to tear that monument down have no earthly idea what it stands for or who those people are. On the other hand, the guys who are standing there saying this is where it absolutely needs to be no matter what are on the other side of the ballpark." You can only remember so much when it comes to the Civil War. You have to choose the memory of slaves or beloved sons. You have to forget someone.

Both Christy Coleman and Bertram Hayes-Davis know what should be done with Silent Sam. He should be moved to a museum or to a Confederate Cemetery, a place of contemplation where the work of history, uncovering the mystery of why people did what they did so that we may understand why people do what they do, may be undertaken. The legislature has rendered the obvious solution impossible. But also, to put these monuments aside would be to fail to reckon with the reality on the ground: For Maya Little and Jake Sullivan, Silent Sam is not some abstruse historical question. The rise and fall of the statue in their midst is lived experience to them. They *want* to relive history. They don't want the compromises of the past. Why would they cherish the disinterested contemplation of history? How much nuance can you tolerate when they try to take away your humanity? How much discussion can

THE END OF THE REPUBLIC

you have when they want to degrade your ancestors? How can you be reasonable when they want to take away your future? How can you be civil when they want to strip away your past?

On December 3, 2018, Chancellor Carol Folt and the UNC board of trustees continued the grand American tradition of impossible compromise when they recommended the construction of a new building on campus to house Silent Sam. The construction was going to cost $5.3 million plus an additional $800,000 in annual operating costs. It was an ingenious answer in a way. If they couldn't put Silent Sam in a museum off campus, they would bring a museum to campus.

The solution satisfied nobody. "Why would our ancestors want their contributions and sacrifices moved from the public square to a place where we will be the only ones to appreciate them?" Jake Sullivan wonders. "Certainly, where the proposal suggests it should go is far out of the way and down by the hospital, where it would see very little related foot traffic. It's essentially just a basement for the university to store what it now considers its trash." For Maya Little, the new building is a direct threat to the student body, since there can be little doubt that there will be violent protests by both sides wherever it is. "Where are they going to build this mausoleum, this shrine for Silent Sam?" she asks. "That's five minutes away from a synagogue. And it's in South Campus, where most Black students continue to live, because UNC still is a very segregated campus." For Sullivan the new building for Silent Sam is a garbage disposal and for Maya Little it's a shrine.

On December 14, the board of governors rejected the proposal anyway. At the time of writing, the question of Silent Sam remains up in the air. The truth is that no compromise was ever possible because of all the compromises America has already made, the compromises by which America built itself, by which it has lived. The forces ripping Americans apart have seams already prepared for the tear. "We're fighting for our lives," Little says. "We're fighting for our dignity. We're going to keep fighting no matter what." Monumental symbols are supposed to bind the past to the future. Silent Sam serves that role faithfully. He watches over the cracks that are opening just as he was supposed to watch over the covering up of the old cracks. The tensions of the American origin remain. It is a double country. Black woman. White man.

Silent Sam was a vicious, fraudulent lie that kept America together. When the lies you tell yourself no longer make sense, how do you live?

The Ongoing Constitutional Crisis

Like any psychotic break, America's current political insanity goes back to its beginnings. The three-fifths clause, debated at the Philadelphia Convention, was right at the heart of the Constitution, right at the heart of the new country. It was the first compromise that should not have been made in a country defined by compromises that should not have been made.

The struggle was over Northern against Southern representation but it was also over the nature of taxation and representation and also over what constituted a human being. Slave states received three-fifths of a vote for every slave in their possession, which increased their taxes but also their power. In the debates on July 12, 1787, founding father Edmund Randolph "lamented that such a species of property exists, but as it did exist the holders of it would require this security." That national lament, a squirming acceptance of recognized evil, began shaping the course of American history right away. Without the three-fifths clause, Jefferson would not have beaten Adams in the election of 1800. Without the three-fifths clause, Virginia would not have controlled the presidency for thirty-two of America's first thirty-six years. The Electoral College, then as now, gave precedence to Southern and reactionary elements that shaped the country.

Slavery and racism are not uniquely American. The British Empire helped to create the transatlantic slave trade, and powerful interests relied on slavery for their wealth and privilege. But the British Empire was not ripped apart by abolition. Brazil was a slave-based economy, importing nearly half of all slaves during the nineteenth century, and it abolished the practice only in 1888. Slavery has left a terrible legacy of cruel degradation in Brazil, but the end of slavery did not require the near destruction of the country. The unique American contradiction is slavery embedded among people celebrating freedom—both impossible and actual. The crisis comes as a question—a question that America refuses to answer: Do Black people count? Because America refuses to answer the question, the question refuses to go away. It is the American question. It is the question that American history has been trying to work out. Do Black people count? The answer America has always given is "sort of." Three-fifths.

The founders, and those who followed them, hoped the whole ugly business of slavery would just go away. Thomas Jefferson embodied his national contradiction to such an extent he amounts practically to an allegory. He was a double man. He hated slavery and lived by it. During the period when he was writing the Declaration of Independence, he described the slave trade as a "cruel war against human nature itself, violating its most sacred rights of life and liberty in the persons of a distant people . . ." He believed that slavery destroyed master as well as slave. "Nothing is more certainly written in the book of fate than that these people are to be free," he wrote. Nonetheless, Jefferson was, as a matter of course, deeply racist, a slaveholder, believing African Americans to be foul-smelling and subject only to "transient" grief. Jefferson preached ideals and impregnated his slaves. His hypocrisy was American to the core. He ate the fruits of slavery but knew the tree was rotten. He wanted life to go on as before and knew that it couldn't. Jefferson believed that the young men who had "sucked in the principles of liberty as if it were their mother's milk" would end slavery in a generation or so.

Inconsistency, not racism, is the American bugbear. For the sake of the Union, in order to remain whole, it compromised on a reality not subject to compromise. The same insoluble mess that faced the framers of the Constitution faces the UNC board of governors. Maya Little's blood and paint, "Black Lives Matter" on one side, and on the other the pride of Jake Sullivan in his ancestors, the tenderness of an established way of life.

At this point in history, 240 years after its composition, much of the US Constitution simply does not apply to reality. Democrats and Republicans alike worship the document as a sacred text, indulging a delirious sentimentality that was the precise opposite of what the framers envisioned as the necessary basis for responsible government. I've seen Trump supporters at rallies with whole chunks written out on the backs of their shirts. During the 2016 election, Gold Star father Khizr Khan waved around a pocket Constitution at a Clinton rally like a talisman to deflect Trump's insults; the *New York Times* reprinted the whole thing, with commentary, like the Talmud. It's absurd. The practice of constitutional law in the United States gives absolute significance to meanings that have long since vanished into history. The geniuses who wrote it, and who signed it less than

100 miles from unclaimed wilderness, never imagined for a moment that their plans for a new republic would survive for 250 years. They were much too sensible. The founders never desired their permanence. It is only their great-great-great-great-great-grandchildren who conjure the founders into gods among men. Americans worship ancestors whose lives were spent overthrowing ancestor worship; they pointlessly adhere to a tradition whose achievement was the overthrow of pointless traditions. Jefferson himself believed it was the "solemn opportunity" of every generation to update the constitution "every nineteen or twenty years." Before Trump and anything he may or may not have done, there was already a constitutional crisis. There is no way to govern rationally when your foundational document is effectively dead and you worship it anyway.

The legitimacy crisis that has infected the American political system can't be resolved with an election. It's not a question of political choices, this president or that president, this party or that party. People are losing faith in the basis of the government of the country. They've already lost faith in their political class. They've nearly lost faith that government can be an instrument of policy. They're starting to lose faith in their history. Faith may sound like a vague and arbitrary foundation. But ultimately faith in its own reality is the substance of any nation.

The United States, if it is to survive, requires a new Constitutional Convention. The loathing overtaking the country makes that possibility more remote every day.

Have the Conditions for Secession Been Met?

In America, more than in any other country in the world, treason is just a matter of dates. "In the long run, all countries are dead," Ryan Griffiths says. "The same will happen to the United States." *The History of the Fall of the American Republic*, author still unborn, will no doubt recognize who and what to blame: the nihilistic hyper-partisanship of Newt Gingrich; Bill Clinton allowing China into the WTO on the mistaken assumption that capitalism and democracy were inevitably linked and that the American middle class would rise on the world's swelling tides; *Bush v. Gore*; the suspension of civil liberties in the aftermath of September 11; the wars in Afghanistan and Iraq; the explicit rejection of the "reality-based community"; the Tea Party; *Citizens United*; Obama's failure to unify on immigration and health care; Mitch McConnell's decision not to consider the appointment of Merrick Garland; the presidency of Donald Trump. And there are thousands upon thousands of politicians who put private and party interests ahead of the interests of the institutions, who developed contempt for government in and of itself and rode contempt to power. Apportioning blame makes for a satisfying game. It's a kind of retrospective partisan politics. Blame misses the point. Blame hides the underlying structural weaknesses.

The conditions necessary for separatism to become real are (1) that there's a will to disunion and (2) that the political differences inside the country amount to distinct identities with geographical boundaries. The will to disunion is not yet a majority position, but it's growing, and it's growing consistently across the country. Partisan identity is now a deeper division than race or religion: See Dispatch Two. The distinct geographical boundaries are not set, but they're simple enough to imagine, given the maps of America's political and cultural divisions.

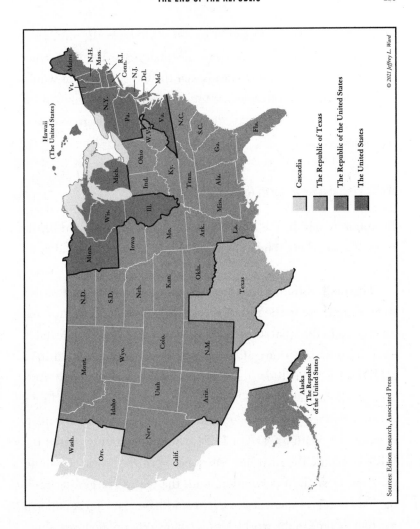

These regions already possess distinct identities, distinct politics, distinct ways of life, and increasingly distinct realities. Obviously, this is nothing more than a rough projection. Border states like Virginia, Georgia, Nevada, and Oklahoma would have to decide by plebiscite where they belong.

But the final requirement for secession would be the most difficult to achieve: goodwill among the negotiating parties. The structure of the United Nations means that the US government would have to let the states that wanted to separate go. The stewards of the United States would have to recognize that their great experiment had ended.

What Would a New North America Look Like?

Disunion would be the death of one country but it would be the birth of four others. These countries would all be sizable and powerful.

The main difference between the American separatist movements and those in the rest of the world is that the countries that emerge from the separation could join the world quite comfortably as independent nations. If Texas were a country, it would have a GDP of $1.59 trillion, tenth in the world, slightly below Brazil and slightly ahead of Canada. It would certainly look like a country, forty-seventh in population, fortieth in size. California is even larger. With a GDP of $2.88 trillion, it recently passed the UK to become the fifth-largest economy in the world. It would rank thirty-sixth in population, with the world's largest technology and entertainment sectors. It would have the largest national median income in the world. Unlike many other regions searching for independence, California and Texas could work as independent countries. Scotland, if it ever left the United Kingdom, would need to belong to NATO and the European Union to ensure its security and its economic viability. The Scottish National Party, in effect, wants to transfer itself to a different superstate from the one it was forced to join in 1707. Quebec separatists believe national sovereignty is required to preserve their survival as a people, but whether or not they belong to Canada, they will still be a tiny French minority in an Anglo continent, with trade and all other matters of importance happening in English. Texas and California share none of those vulnerabilities. California and Texas *are* the new economy. Both states are donor states: they give more in federal taxes than they receive. Military infrastructure wouldn't be a problem, either. California hosts the most active-duty personnel, followed closely by Texas.

The North would not be a superpower anymore but it would continue to be a major power. The economy of the states between Pennsylvania and Maine is the size of Japan's. The South would find itself much poorer and unhealthier and less developed than its neighbors. The federal government currently subsidizes the Southern states considerably. South Carolina alone receives $7.87 back for every dollar in taxes it pays. Life expectancy in the South is considerably shorter than in the rest of the country. Infant mortality rates are much higher. But Florida and Alabama have a combined economy as large as Mexico's, and the twelve Midwestern states produce more than Germany. The citizens of a new Confederacy would find themselves in a much Blacker country than the United States: 55 percent of the African American population lives in the South.

What could these countries become? It's a fascinating proposition. Currently, both sides are hobbled by their affiliation. Outside of the United States, a new Confederacy would be liberated to fulfill its political destiny. It would have to define itself on its own terms, rather than against federal authority. It could re-create itself as a Christian nation, banning abortion and gay marriage outright. It could permit no restrictions on any weaponry. It could end any progressive taxation. It could make government small enough to drown in a bathtub, as the saying goes. The North, for its part, would no longer be hobbled by a political system weighted heavily to rump parties who increasingly don't want government in any form. It could enact meaningful policies on health care, police reform, gun control, and the environment. The Union, as it stands, is preventing both sides from becoming the people they want to be.

And wasn't that always the point of the United States of America? Wasn't it set up to allow people to become who they want to be?

The Loss and the Gain of Separation

Disunion could be liberation. Even without the possibility of a violent civil war, the current state of permanent conflict in the United States makes basic policy more difficult to enact and life harder for its citizens. These four new countries would not be anywhere near as powerful as the current iteration of the United States of America, but they would probably be saner, more normal. It's also worth acknowledging that a grand thing would be lost if the United States disunited.

The American experiment was, at its core, a statement of radical faith in the power of openness to difference. It offers a fantastic piece of dialectic, the permission for contradiction. And the founders went all the way, without exception almost: in religion, in speech, in the structure of power, there would be disagreements. They believed that those disagreements would ultimately lead to deeper truths; that was their faith. "This policy of supplying, by opposite and rival interests, the defect of better motives, might be traced through the whole system of human affairs, private as well as public" was the view of the Federalist Papers. Argument, not conclusion, was the hope of the future. Everyone was entitled to their opinion, and those opinions would not be fixed. It is the essence of equality: to be a human among other humans, entitled to an opinion. Jews and Hindus and Christians and Muslims would coexist. Nobody could have a monopoly on truth. The simple grandeur of this basic proposition is its faith in human nature, expressed politically. It has never been rivaled.

F. Scott Fitzgerald famously said that "the test of a first-rate intelligence is the ability to hold two opposed ideas in mind at the same time, and still retain the ability to function." Everything distinctly American has been a fusion of what should be opposites: North and South, white and Black. Self-determination is a moral state and not simply an economic one. How else would so many new religions, new art forms, be born out of a single country? America is its freedom and its openness, its vast production of stories, seemingly without limit, its generation of new technologies, new religions, constant new ideas, its willingness to embrace the new.

Even if breaking up is the sensible option, even if it's better for ordinary Americans, let's be clear about the stakes here. If the American experiment fails, and it is failing, the world will be poorer, more brutal, lesser. The world needs America. It needs the idea of America, the American faith, even if that idea was only ever a half-truth. The rest of the world needs to imagine a place where you can become yourself, where you can shed your past, where contradictions that lead to genocide elsewhere flourish into prosperity. Now that America is ceding its place of authority, the source of its power is becoming clear. The American empire was built on the story it told itself. It was an empire built, in perhaps its ultimate contradiction, on the belief in self-determination. And now that its story is crumbling under the weight of its contradictions, the world will miss it.

At the heart of tragedy is the tragic flaw: What makes the hero great destroys him. America's tragic flaw is its openness. Perhaps it was a failure right from the start: slave owners preaching freedom and equality. But it would be a lie, an evil lie, to say that the American experiment did not give the world a glorious and transcendent vision of human beings: worth affirming in their differences, vital in their contradiction. That is still a vision of human existence worth fighting for.

Conclusion:
A Note on American Hope

I don't consider the dispatches in this book to be worst-case scenarios. Neither are they best-case scenarios. I have tried, with the best available evidence, to describe, as simply as I can, what is happening. So I hope I will be taken seriously when I say that, even in the current period of darkness, the American hope is real. The power of hope in America should not be discounted by anyone who wants a sensible analysis of its current predicament.

The American experiment has always been an experiment in hope. Hope shines from its face. Hope lives in its guts. The pilgrims on Plymouth Rock were bewildered by hope, a hope not just for prosperity and freedom but for a type of divine reflection on earth, "a shining city on a hill." America has filled itself with new hope all along the way: the eyes turned to the Statue of Liberty, the mothers clutching their babies in the Arizona desert. The world pumps a steady supply of dreamers into the United States even when the United States despises and abuses them. It is the Golden Door.

America's place in the world has always been distinguished by its hope. When its foreign policy descended into cynicism and brutality, it worked like other empires and other nations. But a cynical history of the United States would be an incomplete history. For huge swaths of the world, for much of the nineteenth and twentieth century, America was synonymous with hope. The radical generosity of the Marshall Plan in Europe was unprecedented: for any other people, at any other time, the idea that you would rebuild the economy of an enemy who had attempted to annihilate you would be taken as outright insanity. The Americans tried hope. The hope worked. It's also true that hope has sometimes misled America. After the disaster of the Iraq war, John Bolton upped his naivete with sickening arrogance: "What we should have done is said to the Iraqis: 'You're on your own. Here's a copy of the Federalist Papers. Good luck.'" Obama has been selling hope his whole career; his hope always manages to sell even when it's rotted on the shelf.

None of the crises described in this book are beyond the capacity of Americans to solve. It would be entirely possible for the United States to implement a modern electoral system, to restore the legitimacy of the courts, to reform its police forces, to root out domestic terrorism, to alter its tax code to address inequality, to prepare its cities and its agriculture for the effects of climate change, to regulate and to control the mechanisms of violence. All of these futures are possible. There is one hope, however, that must be rejected outright: the hope that everything will work out by itself, that America will bumble along into better times. It won't. Americans have believed their country is an exception, a necessary nation. If history has shown us anything, it's that the world doesn't have any necessary nations.

The hope for the survival of the United States resides in what I can only describe as its spirit. I understand that American spirit is a rarefied and indistinct phenomenon for such a hardheaded book. It is real even if vague. I have always believed that the most beautiful quality of American life is the way Americans talk to each other. You notice it the moment you arrive from a foreign country. The agents behind the airline counters gossip more freely. The cabbie and his fare argue directions more openly. They don't whisper, the way people do in Cuba. They don't talk placidly and exchange endless nothings like Canadians, either. The frankness of American speech is felt more often than recognized, as much a part of the background as the smell of stale tobacco or running engines in the airport. Americans themselves don't notice the way that they talk because they have this habit of assuming everyone is like they are. It's why so many foreigners, myself included, feel jumbled, both liberated and lost in space, on arrival. Frankness is obvious in the most everyday interactions, but it is political, too, the essence of being a citizen rather than a subject.

The United States needs to recover its revolutionary spirit, and I don't mean that as some kind of inspirational quote. I mean that, if it is to survive, the United States will have to recover its revolutionary spirit. The crises the United States now faces in its basic governmental functions are so profound that they require starting over. The founders understood that government is supposed to work for living people rather than for a bunch of old ghosts. And now their ghostly Constitution, worshipped like a religious document, is strangling the spirit that animated their enterprise, the idea that you mold politics to suit people, not the other way around. Does the country have the humility to acknowledge that its old orders no longer work? Does it have the courage to begin again? As it managed so spectacularly at the birth of its nationhood, the United States requires the boldness to invent a new politics for a new era. It is entirely possible that it might do so. America is, after all, a country devoted to reinvention.

The situation is clear: the system is broken, all along the line. Once again, as before, the hope for America is Americans.

Acknowledgments

The People Who Made This Book Happen

I am deeply grateful to Jofie Ferrari-Adler, my editor, and to PJ Mark, my agent. Without them, you would not be holding this book in your hand.

How I Work, and Who Helps Me to Work

Bits and pieces of this book have previously appeared in essays for *Esquire*, the *Guardian*, the *Globe and Mail*, and the *Walrus*. I am grateful to Jessica Reed, for polishing my ideas and my facts, and I am beyond grateful to David Granger, for everything.

The Necessary One

I couldn't write at all if not for Sarah Fulford.

Sources

Introduction to the Immediate Future of the United States

The figures on the likelihood of a civil war come from a Rasmussen poll from June 27, 2018, and *Foreign Policy*, "What Are the Chances of a Second Civil War?," June 28, 2017, and Georgetown University Politics Civility Poll released October 23, 2019. The figures of deaths by anti-government extremists come from the Anti-Defamation League's Center on Extremism. See their February 2020 report *Murder and Extremism in the United States in 2019*. NASA's accuracy measurements can be found in GISS Surface Temperature Analysis (GISTEMP v4) on the website of the Goddard Institute for Space Studies. On election modelers not believing their own models: "One of the Best Election Models Predicts a Trump Victory. Its Creator Doesn't Believe It," Dylan Matthews, Vox, June 14, 2016. Trump's self-aware quote comes from "Trump: 'I didn't come along and divide this country,'" Fox News, February 16, 2017. Obama's Convention speech is here: "Barack Obama's Remarks to the Democratic National Convention," *New York Times*, July 27, 2004. On *The Day After* as an inspiration for presidential action: Ronald Reagan's diary for October 11, 1983. All descriptions of the Civil War come from William Freehling's *The Road to Disunion*, Volumes 1 and 2, Oxford, UK: Oxford University Press, 1990, 2007. The YouGov poll showing that 88 percent of Republicans believe the election was illegitimate was published on November 19, 2020.

Dispatch One: The Battle of the Bridge

The legal and political details of the struggle have been re-created from the interview with the retired colonel, but several key points also derived from Kevin Benson and Jennifer Weber, "Full Spectrum Operations in the Homeland: A 'Vision' of the Future," *Small Wars Journal*, July 2012.

Lieutenant General Michael Flynn tweeted a full-page ad in the *Wash-*

ington Times on November 30 from the "We the People Convention" that called for the imposition of martial law. See "Calls for martial law and US military oversight of new presidential election draws criticism," *Military Times*, December 2, 2020. On May 31, 2021, Michael Flynn was asked "why what happened in Minamar [*sic*] can't happen here?" he replied "No reason, I mean it should happen here." He later posted a message to a Parler account saying, "There is no reason whatsoever for any coup in America." Vernon Jones made the remark about shooting Biden supporters at a rally on November 5, 2020. Matt Bevin's speech against Hillary Clinton was made on September 13, 2016, at the Values Voters Summit.

The reaction to Jade Helm 15 is described in Manny Fernandez, "As Jade Helm 15 Military Exercise Begins, Texans Keep Watch 'Just in Case,'" *New York Times*, July 15, 2015. The details of bridge repair comes from the American Road & Transportation Builders Association, 2019 Bridge Conditions Report.

The description of Joseph Arpaio's tent cities can be found in Maya Salam, "Last Inmates Leave Tent City, a Remnant of Joe Arpaio," *New York Times*, October 11, 2017, and the description of David Clarke's medals, from Philip Bump, "Here's What the Pins That Sheriff Clarke Wears Actually Mean," *Washington Post*, May 26, 2017.

On the rise of domestic terrorism: Institute for Family Studies, "The Demography of the Alt-Right," August 9, 2018. Center for Strategic and International Studies, "The Escalating Terrorism Problem in the United States," CSIS Briefs, June 17, 2020.

The details on sovereign citizens come principally from the interview with Ryan Lenz. The 2014 survey of law enforcement about the concern over sovereign citizens is referenced in remarks by Assistant Attorney General for National Security John Carlin at a forum at George Washington University, October 14, 2015.

The details of the events at the Malheur National Wildlife Refuge in Oregon can be found at Julie Turkewitz and Eric Lichtblau, "Police Shooting of Oregon Occupier Declared Justified, but F.B.I. Faces Inquiry," *New York Times*, March 8, 2016, and Kirk Johnson, "F.B.I. Agent Told the Truth, Jury Finds. He Did Not Fire His Weapon During Militia Standoff," *New York Times*, August 10, 2018.

The details of the Capitol Hill Autonomous Zone come from Evan Bush, "Welcome to the Capitol Hill Autonomous Zone, Where Seattle Protesters

Gather Without Police," *Seattle Times*, August 12, 2020, and from "The De-mands of the Collective Black Voices at Free Capitol Hill to the Government of Seattle, Washington," published on Medium, June 9, 2020. The details of spiking crime come from Executive Order 2020-08, ordered by Jenny A. Durkan, mayor of Seattle, on June 29, 2020. The comparison of left-wing and right-wing violence can be found in Center for Strategic and International Studies, "The Escalating Terrorism Problem in the United States," CSIS Briefs, June 17, 2020.

The details of hard-right infiltration of law enforcement is mostly from interviews with Michael German, but other details came from his reports for the Brennan Center for Justice, where he is a fellow focusing on Liberty & National Security. See "Confronting Explicit Racism in Law Enforcement," September 4, 2020, and "White Supremacist Links to Law Enforcement Are an Urgent Concern," September 1, 2020. On the hard-right infiltration of the US military, see Leo Shane III, "Signs of White Supremacy, Extremism up Again in Poll of Active-Duty Troops," *Military Times*, February 6, 2020.

On the generals failing to understand the narrative component of war: "Reflection on the 'Counterinsurgency Decade': Small Wars Journal Inter-view with General David H. Petraeus," September 2013.

The gun statistics come from Sabrina Tavernise, "An Arms Race in America: Gun Buying Spiked During the Pandemic. It's Still Up," *New York Times*, May 29, 2021, and Sam Morris, "Mass Shootings in the US: There Have Been 1,624 in 1,870 Days," *Guardian US*, February 15, 2018, and Amanda Michelle Gomez, "DC Recovered 115 Ghost Guns in 2019, up from 25 the Year Before," *Washington City Paper*, January 10, 2020.

The two incidents of dirty bombs can be found in Walter Griffin, "Re-port: 'Dirty Bomb' Parts Found in Slain Man's Home," *Bangor Daily News*, February 10, 2009, and Dan Sullivan, "National Guard 'Neo-Nazi' Aimed to Hit Miami Nuclear Plant," *Tampa Bay Times*, June 13, 2017.

The details of the *JP 3-24* can be found in *Joint Publication 3-24, Counter-insurgency*, April 25, 2018. Validated April 30, 2021.

Dispatch Two: Portrait of an Assassination

On mortality rates in fishing: Jacquelyn Smith, "Fishermen Face the Most Dangerous Work in US," *NBC News*, September 5, 2011. On combat deaths: "Trends in Active-Duty Military Deaths Since 2006," *Congressional Research Service*, May 17, 2021.

The life of Jared Loughner is described in Jo Becker, Serge F. Kovaleski, Michael Luo, and Dan Barry, "Looking Behind the Mug-Shot Grin," *New York Times*, January 15, 2011.

The details on racial resentment derive from the interview with Webster but see also Alan Abramowitz and Jennifer McCoy, "United States: Racial Resentment, Negative Partisanship, and Polarization in Trump's America," Annals, AAPSS, 681, January 2019. Also Dylan Matthews, "One of the Best Election Models Predicts a Trump Victory. Its Creator Doesn't Believe It," Vox, June 14, 2016.

On details of hyper-partisanship: Keith Chen and Ryne Rohla, "The Effect of Partisanship and Political Advertising on Close Family Ties," *Science* 360, 1020–24, June 2018. *Pew Research Report*, "Partisanship and Political Animosity in 2016," June 22, 2016. Kevin Drum, "You Hate Me, Now with a Colorful Chart!," *Mother Jones*, September 27, 2012. Shanto Iyengar and Sean J. Westwood, "Fear and Loathing Across Party Lines: New Evidence on Group Polarization," *American Journal of Political Science* 59:3 (July 2015), 690–707. Anirban Mitra and Debraj Ray, "Implications of an Economic Theory of Conflict: Hindu-Muslim Violence in India," *Journal of Political Economy* 122:4, 2013. US Census, "Demographic Turning Points for the United States: Population Projections for 2020 to 2060," *P25-1144*, Issued March 2018. University of Virginia, Weldon Cooper Center for Public Service, Demographics Research Group, National Population Projections, 2018.

On the celebration of domestic terrorists: Zack Beauchamp, "An Online Subculture Celebrating the Charleston Church Shooter Appears to Be Inspiring Copycat Plots," Vox, February 7, 2019. Matthew Impelli, "Kyle Rittenhouse's Mother Receives Standing Ovation at Wisconsin GOP Event," *Newsweek*, September 25, 2020. Joe Sonka, "Thomas Massie Praises Kyle Rittenhouse, Says He Showed 'Incredible Restraint,'" *Louisville Courier Journal*, September 3, 2020. Lee Rainie and Andrew Perrin, "Key Findings About Americans' Declining Trust in Government and Each Other," Pew Research, July 22, 2019.

Details on Washington: Edward Larson, *The Return of George Washington: Uniting the States, 1783–1789*, New York: William Morrow, 2015.

Dispatch Three: The Fall of New York

The family averages derive from the US Census, 2017.

Maps of the Greater Manhattan Seawall derived from US Army Corps

of Engineers, New York District, https://www.nan.usace.army.mil/Portals
/37/20190308_FINAL_HatsAlt2_AreasBenefitingByFeature.pdf. Map of
surge effects from https://gothamist.com/news/map-nyc-has-new-hurricane
-evacuation-zones.

Description of conditions during Covid Thanksgiving taken from *New
York Times*, November 26, 2020.

On income inequality: Nick Hanauer, "The Pitchforks Are Coming . . .
for Us Plutocrats," *Politico*, July/August 2014. Brian Faler, "Bill Gates Calls
for Higher Taxes on the Rich," *Politico*, January 2020. Estelle Sommeiller
and Mark Price, "The New Gilded Age: Income Inequality in the U.S. by
State, Metropolitan Area, and County," Economic Policy Institute, July 19,
2018.

Manabe, as cited above, on climate models. Leo Hickman, "The Carbon
Brief Interview: Syukuro Manabe," Carbon Brief, July 7, 2015.

On the export values of American commodity crops: "Food Price Vol-
atility a Growing Concern, World Bank Stands Ready to Respond," World
Bank, July 30, 2012. Michael D. Edgerton, "Increasing Crop Productivity to
Meet Global Needs for Feed, Food, and Fuel," *Plant Physiology* 149, no. 1
(January 2009): 7–13.

The details of food changes due to the Great Depression come from Jane
Ziegelman and Andrew Coe, *A Square Meal: A Culinary History of the Great
Depression*, New York: HarperCollins, 2016.

The 300 percent increase in Category 5 hurricanes: "Global Warming
and Hurricanes: An Overview of Current Research Results," Geophysical
Fluid Dynamics Laboratory, March 29, 2021. The size of New York's foreign
exchange: *Triennial Central Bank Survey: Foreign Exchange Turnover in April
2019*, Bank for International Settlements, September 16, 2019.

Facts on Sandy taken from "Hurricane Sandy: Response and Recovery
Progress and Challenges," Special Hearing before the Committee on Appro-
priations, S. HRG, 112-861, Washington, DC: US Government Publishing
Office, 2015.

The model of US migration patterns and the map: Caleb Robinson, Bis-
tra Dilkina, and Juan Moreno-Cruz, "Modeling Migration Patterns in the
USA Under Sea Level Rise," PLOS ONE, January 22, 2020. The stories from
Camp Fire survivors were taken from a Facebook group limited to Camp
Fire survivors, to which the moderator gave me access. For obvious reasons,
their statements will be kept anonymous. On New Orleans, Eleanor Krause

and Richard V. Reeves, "Hurricanes Hit the Poor the Hardest," Brookings Institution, Social Mobility Memos, September 18, 2017.

On the political consequences of Depression: Alan de Bromhead, Barry Eichengreen, and Kevin H. O'Rourke, "Right-Wing Political Extremism in the Great Depression," NBER 17871, DOI 10.3386/w17871, February 2012.

Dispatch Four: The Outbreak of Widespread Violence

On the Republican excuses for insurrection: Brittany Shammas, "A GOP Congressman Compared Capitol Rioters to Tourists. Photos Show Him Barricading a Door," *Washington Post*, May 18, 2021. The Limbaugh quote is recorded at Dominick Mastrangelo, "Limbaugh Dismisses Calls to End Violence After Mob Hits Capitol." *The Hill*, January 7, 2021.

The two incidents of dirty bombs can be found in Walter Griffin, "Report: 'Dirty Bomb' Parts Found in Slain Man's Home," *Bangor Daily News*, February 10, 2009, and Dan Sullivan, "National Guard 'Neo-Nazi' Aimed to Hit Miami Nuclear Plant," *Tampa Bay Times*, June 13, 2017.

The details of the effects of a dirty bomb come from "Radiological Attack: Dirty Bombs and Other Devices," *News & Terrorism, Communicating in a Crisis*, a fact sheet from the National Academies and the US Department of Homeland Security, 2004.

The details of the *JP 3-24* can be found in *Joint Publication 3-24, Counterinsurgency*, April 25, 2018. Validated April 30, 2021.

Daniel Bolger, *Why We Lost: A General's Inside Account of the Iraq and Afghanistan Wars*, New York: Mariner, 2014.

The stats on American military land ownership come from Federal Land Ownership: Overview and Data, Congressional Research Services, Updated February 21, 2020. The statistics on the military economy as a percentage of the GDP comes from the World Bank, 2019. For the number of veterans in the United States, see Katherine Schaeffer, "The Changing Face of America's Veteran Population," Pew Research Center, April 5, 2021. On the monopoly of trust, see Andrew Bacevich, "Why the Military Is Still the Most Trusted Institution in America," NPR, September 27, 2016.

For the economic stats on Biden versus Trump, see Aaron Zitner, "Biden Counties Account for 70% of U.S. GDP," *Wall Street Journal*, November 10, 2020.

The details on the brutality of the wars against Indigenous people come from Robert G. Hays, *A Race at Bay: New York Times Editorials on "the In-*

dian Problem," 1860–1900, Carbondale and Edwardsville: Southern Illinois University Press, 1997.

The details on the Battle of Algiers come from Alistair Horne, *A Savage War of Peace: Algeria, 1954–1962*, New York: Viking, 1978.

Dispatch Five: The End of the Republic

For the number of nations, see Alberto Alesina and Enrico Spolaore, "What's Happening to the Number and Size of Nations?," E-International Relations, November 9, 2015.

For Reuters poll and its effects, see "Journalist Spotlight: Mo Tamman on Reuters Poll on U.S. Citizens' Opinions of State Secession," Reuters, September 24, 2014.

The essays on the possibility of disunion come from Jesse Kelly, "It's Time for the United States to Divorce Before Things Get Dangerous," *The Federalist*, April 10, 2018. Kevin Baker, "It's Time for a Bluexit," *New Republic*, March 9, 2017.

On American nations within a nation: Joel Garreau, *The Nine Nations of North America*, New York: Avon, 1989. Colin Woodard, *American Nations: A History of the Eleven Rival Regional Cultures of North America,* New York: Penguin, 2012. Peter J. Rentfrow, Michal Kosinski, David J. Stillwell, Samuel D. Gosling, Markus Jokela, and Jeff Potter, "Divided We Stand: Three Psychological Regions of the United States and Their Political, Economic, Social, and Health Correlates," *Journal of Personality and Social Psychology*, online October 14, 2013.

For density and elections, see Amy Walter, "Density as Destiny?," *Cook Political Report*, December 2, 2020.

For Richard Florida's comments, see Malcolm Burnley, "Richard Florida Has an Idea About Who Could Win the U.S. Presidency in 2020," *Next City*, April 11, 2017.

On the "Big Sort": Bill Bishop, *The Big Sort: Why the Clustering of Like-Minded America is Tearing Us Apart*, New York: Mariner, 2009.

On support for secession, see Robyn Ross, "Most Likely to Secede," *Texas Monthly*, September 2015. Sharon Bernstein, "More Californians Dreaming of a Country Without Trump: poll," Reuters, January 23, 2017.

For the details on the Texas GOP convention in 2016, see Amber Phillips, "Texas Republicans Have Opted Not to Secede from the United States, After All," *Washington Post*, May 13, 2016. Jerry Brown's remarks were quoted in

Sammy Roth, "California, China Join Forces to Tackle Climate Change," *Desert Sun*, March 4, 2015. For Sessions's remarks, see Josh Gerstein, "Trump Administration Goes on Offense, Sues California over Sanctuary Law," *Politico*, March 6, 2018.

On Scalia, see Ben Smith, "Scalia: No to Secession," *Politico*, February 16, 2020. On the impossibility of constitutional secession, see David A. Strauss, "The New Textualism in Constitutional Law," 66 *George Washington Law Review* 1153 (1997): 1155–56 (1998).

For the details about the support for Silent Sam's restoration and the legislation surrounding it, see Timothy J. Ryan and Marc J. Hetherington, "There Might Be Another Solution for Silent Sam," *Raleigh News & Observer*, November 8, 2018.

For Edmund Randolph's quote, see *The Records of the Federal Convention of 1787*, Volume 1, New Haven, CT: Yale University Press, 1966, p. 594.

On Jefferson's relationships to his slaves, see Henry Wiencek, *Master of the Mountain: Thomas Jefferson and His Slaves*, New York: Farrar, Straus & Giroux, 2012.

The stats on the size of states by GDP are from the Bureau of Economic Analysis at the US Department of Commerce. Tim Smith, "SC Does Better Than Most in Receiving Federal Dollars," *Greenville News*, October 20, 2014. Stats on the Black population in the South come from the 2010 Census.

The quote from the Federalist Papers comes from Federalist Papers No. 51 (1788), The Bill of Rights Institute.

Conclusion: A Note on American Hope

John Bolton's quote came from "Lunch with the FT: John Bolton," *Financial Times*, October 19, 2007.